THE DARK NIGHT *of the* SOUL

The Dark Night of the Soul

by

Georgia Harkness

261

ABINGDON PRESS

Nashville • New York

THE DARK NIGHT OF THE SOUL

Copyright MCMXLV by Whitmore & Stone

Library of Congress Catalog Card Number: 45-3474

Scriptural quotations, unless otherwise indicated, are
from the American Standard Version of the Revised
Bible, copyright renewal, 1929, by the International
Council of Religious Education.

PRINTED AND BOUND BY THE
PARTHENON PRESS, AT NASHVILLE,
TENNESSEE, UNITED STATES OF AMERICA

Acknowledgments

To *The Christian Century* I am indebted for permission to reprint in full two articles, "If I Make My Bed in Hell" (January 14, 1942) and "The Practice of the Presence of God" (January 26, 1944), and to use parts of two others. An article on "The Dark Night of the Soul" in the Summer, 1944, issue of *Religion in Life* has been incorporated, though in segments. Dr. Paul S. Minear has graciously permitted me to use in the Appendix a portion of his brochure *A Preface to the New Testament*. The Association Press is letting me reprint some pages from my Hazen book, *Religious Living*. To my friends Dr. Ernest Fremont Tittle, Rev. Emmett W. Gould, Helen M. Kostka, M.D., and Miss Verna Miller I am most grateful both for helpful suggestions regarding the manuscript and for encouragement in the project.

Contents

Introduction

The Dark Night of the Soul is the title of an important but now little-read book of the sixteenth century by the Spanish mystic St. John of the Cross. It deals with an experience which is not that of a remote time or place, or special degree of saintliness, but which besets the path of the earnest Christian in every age. Its theme is the sense of spiritual desolation, loneliness, frustration, and despair which grips the soul of one who, having seen the vision of God and been lifted by it, finds the vision fade and the presence of God recede.

There are many such, today as always. Spiritual bereftness, or "dryness," is a common theme in the mystical literature of the past, and human nature does not materially alter its pattern with the passage of time. But when one examines the modern literature of religious therapy and psychology of religion, one finds a surprising vacuum in regard to this experience. Much has been written on conversion; there are excellent devotional manuals and books on prayer; a useful literature on the relations of religion to health is being created. The common assumption in such writings is that God is always available to the penitent and surrendered soul. This is what the sufferer wants to believe, but his suffering becomes the more poignant because his experience does not validate it.

This book stems from the conviction that the theme needs to be reopened. It is written primarily for those who have tried earnestly, but unsuccessfully, to find a Christian answer to the problem of spiritual darkness. Among the millions who today "sit in darkness and the shadow of death" there are, of course, many who have never attempted seriously to win spiritual mastery through religious faith. To them the usual doorways to religious power stand open, and these ought resolutely to be entered. But there are also uncounted multitudes who have sought as earnestly as they were able to find power in God, and without apparent success. It is these unhappy ones, who not only continue on in the "dark night" but are plunged still deeper into it by the corroding effects of failure, who are the chief object of our concern. Through frustrated religious hopes not a few have lost faith in God, faith in themselves, and—what is less important but very serious—faith in the Church and its spokesmen. It is time that their case were given fuller consideration.

That this is a life-and-death matter with many persons was brought vividly to my attention some years ago when there appeared in *The Christian Century* an article of mine entitled "If I Make My Bed in Hell." Usually after an article is published I receive a few letters from readers who are moved to express their appreciation or disapproval. On this occasion there were more than ten times the usual number, and I am still getting them from persons who felt that their plight had been stated for them. After due allowances are made for the fact that some correspondents were probably simply bidding for sympathy, there was an unmistakable cry for understanding and help. Some witnessed to a triumphant experience of delivery from depression by God's power; others said that they or their loved ones had sought it in vain. Many asked where they could find further light.

This study presents no final wisdom, but is a further elaboration of the problem with such suggestions as I am able to give from the background of religious thinking. I should have preferred that the book be written by one who has had training in clinical psychology, but it has seemed better to write than to wait. The field is open, and there is room for many.

The first chapter introduces the problem by a reprint of the article above mentioned. Subsequent chapters examine the phenomena of the "dark night," both from classical literature and from current experience. So complex a thing is it that, before we can go further in understanding it, some deep-lying theological issues regarding the problem of evil and the challenge of death have to be considered. Then the causes of the experience, physiological and environmental as well as moral and religious, are canvassed for such light as they throw upon means of deliverance. The remainder of the book attempts to point the way out by the channels of personal religious devotion. Here the reader may find, it is hoped, some suggestions for greater fruitfulness in normal religious living as well as for the conquest of darkness.

There is one assumption without which this quest cannot be undertaken. This is that there is a way forward and out of the dark. One can launch forth with much tentativeness and keep going if he believes that the goal is sure. Failing in this confidence, he finds his springs of action impeded at the outset.

Such assurance we can have through the God revealed in Jesus Christ. It is the ultimate conviction of Christian faith that there is no situation in life where spiritual defeat is final. We may be defeated, but God cannot be. It is the message of Christianity—and has been ever since the first Easter morning—that though God's victory may be deferred it cannot be lost. The way out of spiritual darkness is certain if it is sought by God's strength and in his way. What that way is no human person can fully declare, but God has not left us to wander without direction. Across the years he speaks in Christ to say to darkened spirits in our time, "Let not your heart be troubled, neither let it be afraid." In his light we can see light.

Chapter I

If I Make My Bed in Hell

IT IS, PERHAPS, EFFRONTERY TO SUGGEST THAT THERE IS anything new to say on the problem of evil. Has it not all been said many times, in volumes innumerable and in discussions that, like the stream of pain itself, flow through the ages? I do not claim any great new revelation. However, there is an aspect of the problem I have seldom found recognized in the books and sermons to which I have been exposed through a good many years.

I

Our Christian faith affirms that as workers together with God we can transform some evil situations. Those we cannot transform we must seek to transcend by God's strength. The last word in the problem of evil, whether evil be conceived as sin or as suffering, is not to be found in a theoretical explanation but in the promise repeatedly validated in Christian experience: "My grace is sufficient for thee: for my power is made perfect in weakness."

But is it? Why did the psalmist pray, "Take not thy holy Spirit from me," unless he thought that sometimes the Holy Spirit evaded his most earnest seeking? Why did Jesus in his moment of darkest agony pray, "My

13

God, my God, why hast thou forsaken me?" Why, save that he felt cut off from the face of God at the very moment he needed most to see it? This is the deepest hell—not merely to suffer, but to suffer and seek in vain for God's sustaining presence.

When in quietness and confidence one can say, "If I make my bed in hell, behold, thou art there!" [1] then anything is endurable. With this victorious faith, Christians through the ages have met and conquered affliction. But the depths of the mystery of the problem of evil appear at the point where the Christian does not find this possible. Believing in God, sensitive to his will, seeking earnestly for God's presence, he cries to God out of the depths. And his own words come back to mock him.

Various courses are followed when a person who is deeply troubled tells the minister that he is inwardly upset but religion does not seem to help him. Some counselors, like Job's friends, overtly charge the distraught soul with secret sin. "Look honestly at yourself, and you will find there pride, anger, envy, avarice, sloth, gluttony, lust," the counsel runs—though not, of course, in these words. (It might be well for Protestants to recover a sense of the meaningfulness of these seven deadly sins!) Since the best of us are sinners the challenge is legitimate, and if put in love and faith it may lead to repentance and spiritual victory. It ought always to do so. But the fact is, it sometimes does not. One may earnestly repent and be heartily sorry for his misdoings —and, in self-accusation but without the lifting of his burden, find his hell deeper than before.

[1] Ps. 139:8 (A.V.).

The wise counselor and understanding Christian will put the emphasis on God's forgiveness as the counterpart of man's repentance, on surrender and trust as prerequisite to the lifting by God of a burden that is intolerable. The Christian gospel means, after all, not that we save ourselves by our repentance, but that God saves us when we repent. This ought to be all one needs to say. Yet the fact remains that sometimes persons of deep spiritual sensitivity, earnestly desiring to trust their lives to God's keeping, find they must cry out as did our Lord, "My God, why hast thou forsaken me?" And this worst of all hells may last, not momentarily, but for days, months, years. . . . It is then that "hope deferred maketh the heart sick."

Mind you, I am not talking about those persons who pray in vain to have some suffering removed, some bad situation in their homes or in the larger community corrected. What we are here considering is the more subtle and more terrible torment of sheer inability to find power in God to bear the pain or meet the situation. If one says that this never happens, or that a person is really not a Christian when it happens, one reveals (pardon me for saying so) either blindness or bigotry. Or perhaps both.

It is not the callous sinner who lives in this kind of hell, but the sensitive soul who is caught by the unresolved conflict of his insight and his impotence. Deprived either of spiritual promptings or of the power to follow them by any measure of free consent, one does not find himself in this situation. A person may live sanely in stolid bovine complacency or insanely in a world of psychic delusions, but he does not find himself at the same time pursued by the Hound of Heaven and cut off from God's presence. On the other hand, when one has both the spiritual promptings of the Christian gospel and normal control of his will, the problem does not appear. The way of salvation is assured, for through repentance and surrender one does find forgiveness and power. The Christian way is justified by its fruits, and our preaching is not vain.

It is in situations where a person is free yet bound, sane yet psychically constricted, able to act responsibly in many matters yet in others impotent, that the problem we are considering emerges. I shall suggest three areas in which this occurs, all of which are far more common than is ordinarily recognized.

II

The first of these is in situations where the external environment so presses upon the individual as to limit greatly his capacity for spiritual transcendence over evil. John Bennett, one of the few theologians of our time who have reckoned with this problem, writes:

Persons are blocked by physiological or psychological or environmental conditions so that it is impossible for them to develop the spiritual strength and insight which are essential if they are to overcome evil in their own lives. What are we to say of the feeble-minded child, or of the man of great devotion who, partly because he does not spare himself, suffers a nervous breakdown and ends his life in this world in a kind of hell? Inequality in the distribution of evil handicaps and in the distribution of the power to overcome them is the hardest of all facts to face.[2]

One may extend these suggestions to include many other types of limitation. What of poverty which so depletes physical vitality through malnutrition that one is simply unable to live victoriously? What of enforced drudgery that cramps the spirit and curtails the vision of God? What of prolonged unemployment that cuts the nerve, not only of social usefulness, but even of a once-cherished intimacy with the God in whose name is victory over the worst that men can do? What of those victims of war—homeless, hungry, and distraught—who, having suffered the loss of all things, by that very fact have suffered the greater loss of a sustaining faith? That there are valiant souls who live victoriously under all these conditions should humble and strengthen us. But what of the many who, trying to be Christian amid the gloom, find the light quenched?

That poverty, drudgery, unemployment, and war have bad effects on personality is, of course, nothing new. The social gospel roots in a recognition of their harmfulness to the inner as well as to the outer life of man. But I have yet to discover any extensive consideration of what they do to basic Christian assumptions regarding man's power to transcend all physical evils through spiritual victory.

III

The second area in which the problem emerges is in the field of physical health. That when one is sick he

[2] *Christian Realism*, Scribner's, 1941, p. 183.

lacks normal powers of self-direction and is therefore to be judged charitably is, fortunately, widely recognized. That one can be very sick and still be spiritually victorious is a fact, and it rightly challenges those in health to emulate the courage of the triumphant sufferer. The positive contribution of religious faith to physical health, long recognized at Roman Catholic shrines and in Christian Science reading rooms, is gradually coming home to the Protestant mind and is throwing light on Jesus' miracles of healing. All this is good.

What I do not find so commonly recognized is that there are some types of illness, relatively mild as illnesses go, which by their very nature sap the power of spiritual victory. One may be very ill with cancer, a broken back, or a ruptured appendix, yet feel the presence of God wonderfully sustaining him. One may be well enough to keep walking around and doing his work, yet feel literally "like the devil." That is, he feels as if a devil had caught him and were holding him suspended in a hell of torment. He knows that he ought to trust God and act like a Christian. But the devil has him!

This is not the place to go into an extended discussion of types of physical disease. It must, however, be pointed out that the endocrine glands have a much closer connection with religion than ministers usually will admit. When we first began to hear about "the glands regulating personality," this information was put in such a naturalistic and behavioristic setting that most of the exponents of Christian faith rejected it. Extravagant claims were made which ought to have been rejected. Nevertheless, believing that man is essentially spirit rather than body, one can profitably learn something about the effects of these glands on the spiritual life.

The endocrine system affects the sympathetic nervous system and thus greatly influences the emotions. The power of such bad emotions as anger, jealousy, and worry to upset bodily health and the corresponding curative value of emotional stability and serenity afford an important link between religion and medicine. But this connection between the glands and the emotions works both ways. An unusually able professor of biochemistry has put it thus: "Without muscles you could not walk; without the central nervous system you could not think; without the sympathetic nervous system you could not feel emotions. When the ductless glands are out of order, it is as impossible to achieve victorious spiritual living by an act of will as it would be to walk without legs."

Some people—though not enough people—know that too much thyroid makes one nervous and high-strung and too little makes one sluggish. Gradually we are learning not to brand as sinful irritability or laziness these emotional expressions of a physical disorder. We are learning also something about the effects of such normal glandular changes as those of puberty and pregnancy on emotional attitudes. Religious education has given considerable attention to the relation of the physiological changes of adolescence to religion. Beyond that there is a great field yet to be explored in the relations of endocrinology to religion.

One type of glandular disturbance is of such importance, since it affects half of the human race who reach middle life, that it merits particular attention. In the *Reader's Digest* for November 1941 is an article by Helen Haberman entitled, "Help for Women Over Forty." In this she points out that every year at least eight million women in the United States go through the menopause. Some experience little or no discomfort. But many do, and with these glandular changes there are often acute emotional disturbances. The article states that, through the production of a new synthetic hormone, glandular therapy greatly relieving such symptoms is now available at low cost.

But what of the religious bearing of this experience on the millions of women without adequate medical care? Irritable, depressed, unable to sleep, and tormented by mysterious pains that may strike anywhere in the body, they do not understand themselves. Their husbands and children do not understand them. "What's got into mother? She's cranky and bawls me out for nothing. She cries all over the place. She talks about being a Christian but doesn't act much like one!" These are common enough comments.

She, too, wonders why it is that she neither feels nor acts much like a Christian. If she seeks out her minister for counsel, more than likely he tells her to surrender to God and gain a moral victory. She tries valiantly, not knowing that he has asked of her something as impossible as to walk without legs. Humiliated, baffled, despairing, she decides she has lost her religion and is now losing her mind. In an earlier day, she would have supposed she had committed the unpardonable sin.

IV

A third area, still less understood and more dangerous for the uninformed to tread upon, is in the field of psychic disorders. Not overt insanity, but neuroses and depressions which make a person feel and act abnormally in some matters when he is entirely sane in others, is the major religious problem. I shall speak of but one type, and what I shall say is on the authority of one of the leading psychiatrists of the Middle West.

There is a relatively common disease called "endogenous depression" which has no ascertainable cause either in the environmental situation or in the state of the body. It may strike anybody at any time, though it is found most often in gifted persons, especially those with unique gifts of self-expression and unusual musical ability. Conscientious persons and those inclined to blame themselves get it more often than the irresponsible. If one has it he is in good company, for Abraham Lincoln, Samuel Johnson, Charles Lamb, Tchaikowsky, and Chopin are among those known to have had it! It runs a course of varying duration, usually several months, during which time the victim has periods of intense unhappiness accompanied by exhaustion, inertia, and self-accusation. Meanwhile he either stops work with what is called a nervous breakdown but feels no better for his idleness, or he keeps working with a bold front but wonders why he feels so utterly unlike himself. The disease always terminates. There are drugs by which to relieve the patient's unhappiness; but as no cause is known, so no cure is known by which to hasten its termination.

This is only one of life's many strange phenomena.

I hesitate to state these facts lest readers feeling lazy or blue from overeating or lack of sleep begin to think they have endogenous depression! Yet its religious significance is vital. The sensitive Christian who has this malady—far from finding it banished by trust in God—torments himself the more with self-accusation because he thinks he ought to find serenity and joy through his religion. He has become a self-centered hypochondriac, is thoroughly ashamed of himself, but is unable by will power or prayer to burst the chains of preoccupation with himself. He knows he ought to appreciate his family and friends, but instead feels possessed either by irritation or by a strange apathy. His reason tells him there are things in life to live for, but to his emotions life is meaningless and the future black. He longs for death, and condemns himself for harboring the thought.

If he screws up his courage to confide these thoughts to his minister, what happens? At best, the minister is sympathetic but may be unable to shed much light. At the worst, he tells the sufferer these are sinful thoughts for which God will punish him in hell. The resulting tension only adds to his living hell. There is seldom a competent psychiatrist at hand to tell him he has a disease which will one day cease of its own accord.

V

What are we to make of these facts? I shall summarize briefly what I gather from them.

First, ministers and other religious counselors need to learn enough of physiology and psychology to know when to offer religion as a cure for bodily and psychic disease, and when to send their people to the doctor. It is dangerous business to prescribe without adequate knowledge, whether the prescription be religion or drugs. There are circumstances when sympathy and understanding are worth far more than a religious formula as the cure for psychic ills.

Second, the sort of social health and medical and psychiatric help suggested in these examples ought to be made accessible to all persons. It is a major part of the Christian enterprise to see that this is done. The social gospel has a long way to go before all the sons and daughters of God can have the alleviation now enjoyed by the privileged few.

Third, the Christian gospel interpreted in love and accepted in faith is relevant to every human situation. There are some things it will not do: let us not make for it unwarranted claims. There is much that it will do, as the saints and seers attest. Let us not grow weary or timid in proclaiming our faith.

Finally, let us trust God, not less but more, with knowledge of these facts. All that has been said in this article but illustrates the infinite complexity of God's world. And whether we find him near or far or feel ourselves cut off from his presence, this is still our Father's world! Though we cannot find God, he finds us. When we are assured that God ceases not to love us, we can watch through the night and wait for the dawn to see his face. We can make our bed in hell—far deeper hells than in our self-confidence we had ever dreamed existed—yet know that he is there.

Such assurance is a faith that is dearly bought, but it is a faith that overcomes the world.

Chapter II

What Is the Dark Night?

THE EXPERIENCE OF THE DARK NIGHT OF THE SOUL IS a common theme in mystical literature. Not only St. John of the Cross but his teacher and comrade in spiritual reform, St. Teresa of Avila, describes with great vividness the soul's bereftness during periods of struggle to recapture the lost sense of God's nearness. Before their time, in the fourteenth century, John Tauler, St. Catherine of Siena, and Henry Suso (whose victory over it caused him to go down in history as the "Blessed Henry Suso") had to fight such darkness. In the seventeenth, George Fox's "great openings" are not to be understood with any clarity except as they are viewed against the backdrop of his great depressions, and John Bunyan had his own battles with the powers of darkness. A detailed and ingenious self-revelation is to be found in Madame Guyon's *Autobiography* and her *Spiritual Torrents*. Times of spiritual "dryness" were apparently the normal expectancy of most of the mystics, and are treated with much understanding and helpful counsel by the author of the *Imitation of Christ*. As *accidie*, or spiritual torpor, the experience was common enough to be regarded by the medieval church as one of the seven deadly sins, the deadliness of which has been obscured in translation by the colorless and inaccurate "sloth."

It may be profitable to outline further the general features of this experience. We shall then examine the testimony of some historic figures and of some present-day sufferers to see its bearing on personality as a whole.

I

The most characteristic note in all descriptions of this unhappy state is that of a frustrated quest for the divine Presence. One who has found in God precious companionship desires to go on to more intimate spiritual fellowship and finds, to his great dismay, that he seems to be further from God than before. To some of the mystics this experience came with sudden shock; in others there was a gradual breaking up of an earlier equilibrium, with "dry times" of increasing duration and frequency encroaching on the life of devotion and sapping its power. The resulting privation threw the soul into confusion, turmoil, and deep distress.

It is important to distinguish this state from that of unregenerate indifference. When one has made no serious attempt to find God, he may be either callously apathetic or acutely unhappy through lack of inner stability, but he does not "lie awake in the dark and weep for his sins." The devout soul in the "dark night" not only weeps for his sins but weeps because he is unable to find in God the release from them that he formerly thought he had. It is also to be distinguished from atheism, for the mystics who came through this experience and looked backward to tell about it give no evidence of having lost their faith in God. What they doubted was not God's existence or his grace but their own ability either to find his presence or to merit his mercy.

A second and closely related characteristic is a union of self-distrust with self-condemnation. "It is an amazing thing," says Madame Guyon, "for a soul that believed herself to be advanced in the way of perfection, when she sees herself thus go to pieces all at once."[1] St. Catherine of Siena, tormented by visions of sin that appalled her, speaks graphically of "digging up the root of self-love with the knife of self-hatred."[2] Many a minister, if he is honest with himself, finds an echo in his soul to the question Suso found God putting to him, "Where then is your resignation? Where is that equal humor in joy and in tribulation which you have so lightly taught other men to love?"[3] The literature dealing with the "dark night" reflects relatively little tendency to put the blame for trouble on outward circumstances, much self-accusation and disgust with one's self for lack of Christian fortitude. Though this is doubtless a form of emotional insecurity not unmixed with self-pity, it is not the self-exonerating, alibi-seeking insecurity of the unregenerate.

A third dominant trait is loneliness, which means the bitterness of isolation both from God and man. Bereft of divine companionship, the soul cries out for human fellowship. But this too is denied. Partly because the ex-

[1] *Spiritual Torrents*, I, vii, 2.
[2] *Dialogue*, lxiii.
[3] *Little Book of Eternal Wisdom*, xl. Quoted by Evelyn Underhill in *Mysticism*, p. 492.

perience makes the sufferer irritable and "odd," partly because his increased self-centeredness makes him abnormally sensitive, his friends withdraw. They do not understand him or he them, and he suffers acutely from imagined gibes and slights. Thus he cuts himself off from fellowship just when he needs it most.

A fourth note, following inevitably from the others, is spiritual impotence. This does not mean, for the most part, yielding to overt temptation. The mystics, even in their darkest hours, were usually able to resist the devil when he came in the form of fleshly lusts. What they could not master was the temptation to spiritual weariness and discouragement. They could not rise to the challenge to "be not weary in well-doing," for the soul was already faint and saw no prospect of reaping. Almost invariably a soul caught in the "dark night" thinks that it will never emerge. Madame Guyon speaks for many—and points to an important avenue of release—when she says: "The good appeared to me evil; and—that which is terrible—it seemed to me that this state must last forever. For I did not believe it to be a state, but a true falling away. For if I had been able to believe that it was a state, or that it was necessary or agreeable to God, I should not have suffered from it at all." [4]

Various evil moods ensue, not the least of which is the exasperation of helplessness. Teresa, saint though she was, speaks language understood by the rest of us when she says, "The devil then sends so offensive a spirit of bad temper that I think I could eat people

[4] *Autobiography,* xxiii.

up!" [5] Many who record such spiritual turmoil were victims of ill health, though whether the physical accompaniment was cause or effect it is hard to say. Not infrequently there is evidence of loss of intellectual power and grasp of worldly affairs. In short, the futility which the saints feared often passed from imagination to reality as the state progressed.

II

Though these phenomena may be analyzed point by point, they beset the whole man and cannot be understood apart from their influence on the total personality.

St. John of the Cross emphasizes the purgative character of the experience and its source in the divine will. Nevertheless, none has written more graphically than he of the acute agony of the person caught in its toils. We find him saying:

When the soul is indeed assailed by this Divine light, its pain, which results from its impurity, is immense; because, when this pure light assails the soul in order to expel its impurity, the soul feels itself to be so impure and miserable that it believes God to be against it, and thinks that it has set itself up against God. . . . And what gives it most pain is that it thinks it will never be worthy and that its good things are all over for it. . . .

The second way in which the soul suffers pain is by reason of its weakness, natural, moral and spiritual; for, when this Divine contemplation assails the soul with some strength in order to strengthen it and subdue it, it suffers such pain in its weakness that it nearly swoons away. . . . Sense and spirit, as

[5] *Life,* xxx, 15.

if beneath some immense and dark load, are in such great pain and agony that the soul would find advantage and relief in death. . . .

Beneath the power of this oppression and weight the soul feels itself so far from being favored that it thinks, and correctly so, that even that wherein it was wont to find some help has vanished with everything else, and that there is none who has pity upon it. . . .

What the sorrowful soul feels most in this condition is its clear perception, as it thinks, that God has abandoned it, and in His abhorrence of it has flung it into darkness. . . . For indeed, when this purgative contemplation is most severe, the soul feels very keenly the shadow of death and the lamentations of death and the pains of hell, which consist in its feeling itself to be without God, and chastised and cast out, and unworthy of Him; and it feels that He is wroth with it. All this is felt by the soul in this condition—yea, and more, for it believes that it is so with it forever.

It feels, too, that all creatures have forsaken it, and that it is contemned by them, particularly by its friends.[6]

Already the reader may be saying, "But these saints were morbid creatures! If they had snapped out of themselves and had a happy family life all this could have been avoided." As William James tells us in *The Varieties of Religious Experience*, the struggles of the "sick soul" are always apt to seem morbid to the person who has never had them. But if one is disposed to dismiss such anguish, either scornfully or semi-sympathetically, as the meanderings of a diseased mind, it is well to remember that most of the persons cited *were* saints. In fact, they were greater Christians than most of us

[6] *The Dark Night of the Soul*, II, v, 5-7; vi, 2-3.

will ever be! And again a word from William James is in order: "Here is the real core of the religious problem: Help! help! No prophet can claim to bring a final message unless he says things that will have a sound of reality in the ears of victims such as these." [7]

Let us turn, therefore, to the witness of some prophets and seers whose religious insight and resultant service to humanity are scarcely subject to question.

III

There is little of this experience in the New Testament. The burden of sin so graphically set forth by Paul in the seventh chapter of Romans is not a true case of the dark night, for it was a burden lifted by God on the Damascus Road and Paul's dominant note thereafter is one of triumphant rejoicing and hope. However we interpret Jesus' poignant cry from the cross, "My God, my God, why hast thou forsaken me?" the prevailing temper of his life was certainly not that of divine abandonment, but of divine companionship. These facts place a large question mark after the contention of St. John of the Cross that the dark night is God's gift to those souls whom he most desires to purify and draw to the light of his presence.

But, though neither normative nor desirable from the standpoint of the most authentic Christian experience, the sense of divine abandonment is a common accompaniment of religious sensitivity. One finds it in many of the psalms. There is, for example, the psalm of which Jesus from the cross quotes the opening words:

[7] *The Varieties of Religious Experience*, Longmans, 1902, p. 162.

My God, my God, why hast thou forsaken me?
Why art thou so far from helping me, and from the words
   of my groaning?
O my God, I cry in the daytime, but thou answerest not;
And in the night season, and am not silent.[8]

To interpret this cry from the cross as a paean of triumph, since Jesus quotes the first line of a psalm that ends triumphantly, seems to me quite unrealistic, and altogether too facile an explanation. Had he wished to express triumphant assurance of God's abiding presence, a far more appropriate expression than the twenty-second psalm would have been the first line of the twenty-third or the forty-sixth. If the record is authentic, the most natural interpretation is that what Jesus quoted is what he felt in that dark moment of acute spiritual anguish. The triumph appears, not here, but in another and more ultimate word, "Father, into thy hands I commend my spirit."

St. John of the Cross cites numerous passages from the psalms to show the meaning of the dark night. Among them are:

My soul thirsteth for thee, my flesh longeth for thee,
In a dry and weary land, where no water is.[9]

I was dumb with silence, I held my peace, even from good;
And my sorrow was stirred.
My heart was hot within me.[10]

I remember God, and am disquieted:
I complain, and my spirit is overwhelmed.

[8] Ps. 22:1-2.   [9] Ps. 63:1.   [10] Ps. 39:2-3.

31

Thou holdest mine eyes watching:
I am so troubled that I cannot speak.[11]

The double bereftness of separation from God and from human companionship appears in the following:

I am as a man that hath no help,
Cast off among the dead,
Like the slain that lie in the grave,
Whom thou rememberest no more,
And they are cut off from thy hand.
Thou hast laid me in the lowest pit,
In dark places, in the deeps.
Thy wrath lieth hard upon me,
And thou hast afflicted me with all thy waves.
Thou hast put mine acquaintance far from me;
Thou hast made me an abomination unto them:
I am shut up, and I cannot come forth.[12]

Guileless of knowledge of historical criticism, St. John of the Cross assumed such passages to be descriptive of David's journey through the dark night. Whatever may be back of these words, there is a poignancy here that is not to be dismissed with the assumption that they describe an irreligious attitude. If the psalmist had not loved and revered God so much, his soul would not have thirsted for God in a dry and weary land.

There is nowhere in the Old Testament a more tragic, triumphant figure than Jeremiah. He knew well enough in his own experience what the dark night of the soul means. Betrayed by his own townsmen, thrown into a

[11] Ps. 77:3-4.   [12] Ps. 88:4-8.

miry cistern, repeatedly subjected to indignity and danger by the very people for whom he sought to intercede, and apparently abandoned at times even by God, he nevertheless felt a "burning fire shut up in his bones" that would not let him rest till he spoke the word that God gave him to utter. His was a powerful life, but hardly a happy one. Listen to his lament:

Woe is me, my mother, that thou hast borne me a man of strife and a man of contention to the whole earth! . . .

O Jehovah, thou knowest; remember me, and visit me, and avenge me of my persecutors; take me not away in thy longsuffering: know that for thy sake I have suffered reproach. Thy words were found, and I did eat them; and thy words were unto me a joy and the rejoicing of my heart: for I am called by thy name, O Jehovah, God of hosts. I sat not in the assembly of them that make merry, nor rejoiced; I sat alone because of thy hand; for thou hast filled me with indignation.

Why is my pain perpetual, and my wound incurable, which refuseth to be healed? wilt thou indeed be unto me as a deceitful brook, as waters that fail? . . .

I am become a laughingstock all the day, every one mocketh me. . . . Cursed be the day wherein I was born. . . . Wherefore came I forth out of the womb to see labor and sorrow, that my days should be consumed with shame? [13]

It would be hard to find a more perfect expression of the pathos of the dark night. Fidelity to God that seems unrequited, loneliness, misunderstanding, the pass-

[13] Jer. 15:10, 15-18; 20:7, 14, 18.

ing of former joys, the loss of hope, the longing for death—all are here in a few words with startling vividness.

Jeremiah, by any human reckoning, should have been defeated by these attitudes. In our day he would have been charged with having a "manic-depressive psychosis." Yet, having outlasted all of his calumniators, he lives today among the immortals.

It is in the book of Job that the problem is wrestled with most acutely, though the emphasis on Job's loss of possessions and family and his physical affliction overshadows in the drama his spiritual pain. The book was written to disprove the current Hebraic idea that piety insures immunity from suffering, and we rightly put the major emphasis on the great spiritual vision that came to Job from the Whirlwind Voice in lieu of a theoretical explanation of the mystery of pain. However, it is to get but one side of the picture to quote, "I know that my redeemer liveth," [14] or "Though he slay me, yet will I trust in him," [15] or

> I had heard of thee by the hearing of the ear;
> But now mine eye seeth thee.[16]

One catches the overtones of a cosmic spiritual anguish in

> But man is born unto trouble,
> As the sparks fly upward.[17]

[14] Job 19:25.
[15] Job 13:15 (A.V.).
[16] Job 42:5.
[17] Job 5:7.

Yet this generalization does not lay bare the stark misery and rebellion of Job's soul as does the stormy outcry against God that appears in the seventh chapter. Who but a tense, sleepless, bitterly frustrated soul could say:

> So am I made to possess months of misery,
> And wearisome nights are appointed to me.
> When I lie down, I say,
> When shall I arise, and the night be gone?
> And I am full of tossings to and fro unto the dawning
> of the day.
>
> . . . .
>
> My days are swifter than a weaver's shuttle,
> And are spent without hope.
> Oh remember that my life is a breath:
> Mine eye shall no more see good.
> The eye of him that seeth me shall behold me no more;
> Thine eyes shall be upon me, but I shall not be.
> As the cloud is consumed and vanisheth away,
> So he that goeth down to Sheol shall come up no more.
>
> . . . .
>
> Therefore I will not refrain my mouth;
> I will speak in the anguish of my spirit;
> I will complain in the bitterness of my soul.
> Am I a sea, or a sea-monster,
> That thou settest a watch over me?
>
> When I say, my bed shall comfort me,
> My couch shall ease my complaint;
> Then thou scarest me with dreams,
> And terrifiest me through visions:
> So that my soul chooseth strangling,
> And death rather than these my bones.

I loathe my life; I would not live alway:
Let me alone; for my days are vanity.

What is man, that thou shouldest magnify him,
And that thou shouldest set thy mind upon him,
And that thou shouldest visit him every morning,
And try him every moment?
How long wilt thou not look away from me,
Nor let me alone till I swallow down my spittle? [18]

Let me alone! Let me sleep! At least, let me alone till
I can spit! Does not this sound like a modern neuras-
thenic? But with the difference that the protest is directed, not against one's friends or other members of the
household, but against God. The abyss of Job's misery
lies in the fact that God the Redeemer has become God
the Enemy.

Job's friends, of course, were startled and shocked.
Bildad the Shuhite tried both to comfort and to rebuke
him:

Doth God pervert justice?
Or doth the Almighty pervert righteousness?

.   .   .   .

If thou wouldest seek diligently unto God,
And make thy supplication to the Almighty;
If thou wert pure and upright:
Surely now he would awake for thee,
And make the habitation of thy righteousness pros-
    perous.[19]

[18] Job 7:3-4, 6-9, 11-19.
[19] Job 8:3, 5-6.

But Job was not convinced—then. Nor would you have been, in his state of spiritual agony! What Job's friends said to him was in effect what multitudes of baffled but well-meaning counselors have said to distressed souls. "Trust God and don't worry. There's sin in you somewhere. Clean up and God will make everything right." And the words have fallen on deaf ears, or on souls raw with nervous tension. If Job had had something less public than the ash heap as the scene of his misery, he would have fled to his room, slammed the door, and wept into his pillow. Or, if that seems too feminine an expression of his manly exasperation, say instead that he would have cursed roundly and gone home to belabor his wife.

Chapter III

An Ocean of Darkness

IN THE PRECEDING CHAPTER WE LOOKED AT THE PHE-
nomena of the dark night in Jeremiah and Job, and in
the experience of some of the great saints of the Roman
Catholic Church. But what of the Protestant road to
faith, with its greater flexibility and variety of access
to God? Let us observe some famous cases, then some examples from our own time.

There are two eccentric geniuses in the Protestant
tradition whose stories seem made for this kind of study.
Both had overwhelming periods of depression, both
overcame them to the point of becoming apostles whose
Christian witness is still influential, and both left detailed accounts of their spiritual meanderings. These are
George Fox and John Bunyan.[1]

I

George Fox, in his *Journal*, written in Worcester Jail
when he was about fifty, gives an unusually clear account of the "great trouble and temptation" that came

[1] The reader will find accounts of the experience of both Fox and Bunyan
in William James's *The Varieties of Religious Experience,* and in Anton T. Boisen's
The Exploration of the Inner World.

upon him as a young man and of his subsequent release through the "great opening" that came to him from God. With due allowance for the distortion of memory, the story is revealing and has the ring of authenticity.

In childhood he had "a gravity and stayedness of mind and spirit not usual in children"—a suggestion, perhaps, of abnormal seriousness. But no special distress emerged until, at nineteen, he experienced an emotional shock at being urged to drink at a fair by two professing Christians. He became sleepless, walked tensely up and down, sought to be alone, cried much to the Lord. At what he believed to be the command of God, he left his family to become a solitary wanderer. From this point on we had better let him tell his own story:

As I thus traveled through the country, professors [2] took notice of me and sought to be acquainted with me; but I was afraid of them, for I was sensible that they did not possess what they professed.

Now during the time I was at Barnet, a strong temptation to despair came upon me. Then I saw how Christ was tempted, and mighty troubles I was in. Sometimes I kept myself retired in my chamber, and often walked solitary in the Chase there, to wait upon the Lord. I wondered why these things should come to me; and I looked upon myself and said, "Was I ever so before?" Then I thought, because I had forsaken my relations I had done amiss against them; so I was brought to call to mind all my time that I had spent, and to consider whether I had wronged any. But temptations grew more and more, and I was tempted almost to despair, and when Satan

[2] Fox's word for professing Christians.

could not effect his design upon me that way, he laid snares for me and baits to draw me to commit some sin, whereby he might take advantage to bring me to despair.

I was about twenty years of age when these exercises came upon me; and I continued in that condition some years, in great troubles, and fain I would have put it from me. I went to many a priest to look for comfort, but found no comfort from them. . . .

After some time I went into my own country again, and was there about a year, in great sorrows and troubles, and walked many nights by myself. . . .

Now, though I had great openings, yet great trouble and temptation came many times upon me; so that when it was day I wished for night, and when it was night I wished for day. . . .

I fasted much, and walked abroad in solitary places many days, and often took my Bible, and went and sat in hollow trees and lonesome places till night came on; and frequently in the night walked mournfully about by myself; for I was a man of sorrows in the times of the first workings of the Lord in me.[3]

Apparently this sorrowful state was not continuous. Like most victims of the dark night there were times when he felt like his old self, and even had great joy.

Though my exercises and troubles were very great, yet were they not so continual but that I had some intermissions, and was sometimes brought into such a heavenly joy that I thought I had been in Abraham's bosom.[4]

The resolution of his conflict came through a recog-

[3] *Journal,* i.   [4] *Ibid.*

nition of the inadequacy of human sources of help, in conjunction with what he believed to be the direct voice of God. His break with the "priests and preachers" that could not help him is tinged with self-righteousness, but it is illumined also by a sense of divine vocation to preach to others the need of inward change in the way God had opened it to him. This is his graphic account of his deliverance:

But as I had forsaken the priests, so I left the Separate preachers also, and those called the most experienced people; for I saw there was none among them all that could speak to my condition. And when all my hopes in them and in all men were gone, so that I had nothing outwardly to help me, nor could I tell what to do; then, oh, then, I heard a voice which said, "There is one, even Christ Jesus, that can speak to thy condition"; and when I heard it, my heart did leap for joy. . . .

About this time there was a great meeting of the Baptists at Broughton in Leicestershire, with some that had separated from them; and people of other notions went thither, and I went also. . . . The Lord opened my mouth, and the everlasting truth was declared amongst them, and the power of the Lord was over them all. For in that day the Lord's power began to spring, and I had great openings in the Scriptures. . . .

I went back into Nottinghamshire, and there the Lord showed me that the natures of those things, which were hurtful without, were within, in the hearts and minds of wicked men. I cried to the Lord, saying, "Why should I be thus, seeing I was never addicted to commit these evils?" and the Lord answered that it was needful I should have a sense of all conditions, how else should I speak to all conditions, and in this I saw the infinite love of God. I saw also that there was an ocean of darkness and death, but an infinite ocean of light and love which flowed over the ocean of darkness. In that also I saw the infinite love of God; and I had great openings. . . .

I was very much altered in countenance and person, as if my body had been new-moulded or changed. . . . My sorrows and troubles began to wear off, and tears of joy dropped from me, so that I could have wept day and night with tears of joy to the Lord, in humility and brokenness of heart. I saw into that which was without end, and things which cannot be uttered, and of the greatness and infiniteness of the love of God, which cannot be expressed by words. For I had been brought through the very ocean of darkness and death, and through and over the power of Satan, by the eternal, glorious power of Christ.[5]

In the last paragraph lies the key to Fox's subsequent power to endure victoriously not only imprisonment but almost continual misunderstanding, railing, and abuse, and to undergo physical strains that would have killed a dozen ordinary men. It would be too much to contend that Fox was always thereafter sweet and Christlike! He could be harsh toward those who disagreed with him, and his *Journal* is spiced with satire and invective toward the "professors" and "hireling priests." Yet he had the passion for relief of suffering and correction of injustice, the basic democracy, the practice of nonviolence, and the confident trust in the leading of the Inner Light that have made the Society of Friends so great a power in the past three centuries.

[5] *Ibid.*

One hesitates to imagine what the world would have lost if God had not given to George Fox his "great opening."

Before we leave his story we must ask, "Did his depression ever return?" The answer is that it did, though not seriously for the next twenty years. He had what modern psychiatrists call "mood swings," but in spite of them went on with his work, sustained and led by God. There came a time, however, when sympathy with his persecuted fellow Quakers, probably augmented by overwork and inadequate care of health, laid him low.

Again we shall let him tell his story:

As I was walking down a hill, a great weight and oppression fell upon my spirit. I got on my horse again, but the weight remained so that I was hardly able to ride. At length we came to Rochester, but I was much spent, being so extremely laden and burdened with the world's spirits that my life was oppressed under them. . . .

Here I lay, exceeding weak, and at last lost both hearing and sight. Several Friends came to me from London; and I told them that I should be as a sign to such as would not see, and such as would not hear the truth. . . .

Under great sufferings, and groanings, and travails, and sorrows, and oppressions, I lay for several weeks, whereby I was brought so low and weak in body that few thought I could live. . . .

I went to the widow Dry's, where I lay all that winter, warring with the evil spirits of the world, and could not endure the smell of any flesh meat. Persecution was stirred up and wicked Informers set to work, so that a Friend could hardly speak a few words in a private family before they sat down to eat meat, but some were ready to inform against them.

It was a cruel, bloody, persecuting time, but as persecution began to cease I began to arise out of my sufferings. Many precious Friends came far and near to see me and attended upon me; and towards the Spring I began to recover and to walk up and down, to the astonishment of Friends and others.[6]

This recurrence of mental illness, here with acute physical accompaniments, may seem like an anticlimax to the story. One would like, perhaps, to believe that, with Fox's great illumination and surrender, God cured him finally and completely. But life is not always that way. There is no immunity from either physical or spiritual pain. A servant of the Lord may suffer through the dark night, be gloriously delivered from it, and be plunged into it again.

What caused Fox's second great depression? In part, the very ardor of his service of God. In part, doubtless, an unregenerate animus toward those who opposed him and his movement. Could he have been spared the recurrence if his spirit had been better? We do not know. What we do know is that a relapse does not need to mean frustration. As there is no immunity from trouble for the servants of God, so is there no final defeat.

II

John Bunyan's experiences were more abnormal than those of Fox, and had he not become the author of an immortal classic of the soul, he might be dismissed as "a psychopathic." Yet nobody who could write *Pil-*

[6] *Ibid.*, xx.

grim's Progress can be esteemed lightly. His spiritual autobiography is found in *Grace Abounding to the Chief of Sinners,* written like Fox's *Journal* from prison.

His trouble started apparently in childhood, when he tells us he did much swearing, was tormented with thoughts of hell-fire, and had frightful dreams. He accuses himself of "all manner of vice and ungodliness" in his adolescence, though swearing and Sabbathbreaking are the only specific offenses he mentions. At twenty he married. Not long after this, while listening to a sermon on Sabbathbreaking, he fell under conviction of sin; but this did not keep him from engaging in sports and games as usual in the afternoon. Bunyan's first great religious experience came under unusual circumstances:

But the same day, as I was in the midst of a game of Cat, and having struck it one blow from the hole, just as I was about to strike it the second time, a voice did suddenly dart from heaven into my soul, which said, *"Wilt thou leave thy sins and go to heaven or have thy sins and go to hell?"* At this I was put to an exceeding maze; wherefore leaving my cat upon the ground, I looked up to heaven and it was as if I had, with the eyes of my understanding, seen the Lord Jesus looking down on me, as being very hotly displeased with me, and as if he did very severely threaten me with some grievous punishment for these and other ungodly practices.

I had no sooner thus conceived in my mind, but, suddenly, this conclusion was fastened upon my spirit, . . . *that I had been a great and grievous sinner, and that it was now too late for me to look after heaven; for Christ would not forgive me nor pardon my transgressions.* Then I fell to musing on this also; and while I was thinking of it, and fearing lest it should be so, I felt my heart sink in despair, concluding that it was too late; and therefore I resolved in my mind I would go on in sin; for, thought I, if the case be thus, my state is surely miserable; miserable if I leave my sins and but miserable if I follow them. I can but be damned, and if I must be so, I had as good be damned for many sins as be damned for few.[7]

The conflict implied in the statement that he would be miserable if he left his sins and miserable if he followed them becomes the keynote of his struggle for the next few years. He underwent some outward reformation, which led the neighbors to take him to be "a very godly man, a new and religious man." Yet in retrospect he says that at this time he "knew not Christ, nor grace, nor faith, nor hope." He continued to be tormented by fears of hell and anxiety about his salvation, beset by doubts as to whether he was of the elect. Sometimes he had "a very great softness and tenderness of heart"; again he felt overwhelmingly impelled to commit the unpardonable sin. He graphically describes his conflict thus:

All this while, as to the act of sinning, I was never more tender than now. My hinder parts were inward. I durst not take a pin or stick, though but so big as a straw; for my conscience now was sore, and would smart at every touch. I could not now tell how to speak my words, for fear I should misplace them. Oh, how gingerly did I then go, in all I did or said! I found myself as on a miry bog, that shook if I did but stir, and was, as there, left both of God and Christ, and the Spirit, and all good things.[8]

[7] *Grace Abounding*, pars. 22-23.
[8] *Ibid.*, par. 83.

After a year or more of such acute conflict Bunyan found temporary relief through the fellowship of some religious people at Bedford, the preaching and friendship of a minister who trusted him beyond appearances, and the reading of Luther's commentary on Galatians. Of this book he says in a poignant testimony:

God, in whose hands are all our days and ways, did cast into my hand one day a book of Martin Luther's; it was his Comment on the Galatians, . . . the which when I had but a little way perused, I found my condition in his experience, so largely and profoundly handled, as if his book had been written out of my heart.[9]

The journey through the Slough of Despond ought to have ended here. But life has a way of doing the unexpected. As has happened to many another troubled soul, Bunyan found himself before long back where he was before—and in some respects in a worse plight than before.

Though the primary characteristic of the earlier disturbance was an abnormally tender and suggestible conscience, Bunyan now became clearly the victim of obsessions. He felt himself continually tormented by the devil, who at one time would bid him to "sell Christ," at another would drive him away from his meals to pray, "so counterfeit holy also would this devil be." The battle in his soul centered in rival texts of Scripture which seemed to strive for mastery in his mind, comforting texts contending with those that condemned him. The two which epitomized the conflict were "My

[9] *Ibid.*, par. 130.

grace is sufficient for thee" and the words about Esau's selling his birthright for a mess of pottage. The result was a rapid, and what must have been a very disrupting, alternation of moods. We find him saying:

By these words (My grace is sufficient for thee) I was sustained, yet not without exceeding conflicts, for the space of seven or eight weeks; for my peace would be in it, and out, sometimes twenty times a day; comfort now, and trouble presently; peace now, and before I could go a furlong, as full of fear and guilt as ever heart could hold. And this was not only now and then, but my whole seven weeks' experience; for this about "the sufficiency of grace," and that about Esau's parting with his birthright, would be like a pair of scales within my mind; sometimes one end would be uppermost, and sometimes again the other; according to which would be my peace or trouble.[10]

The resolution of the conflict was a peculiar device, though beneath it is to be discerned Bunyan's fundamental faith and sanity in letting the grace of God prove itself. He began to desire the two texts to meet in his mind, not alternately but simultaneously, to see which would get the better of him. The wish being father to the act, it happened. Says he:

Well, about two or three days after, so they did indeed; they bolted both upon me at a time, and did work and struggle strangely in me for a while; at last that about Esau's birthright began to wax weak, and withdraw, and vanish; and this about the sufficiency of grace prevailed with peace and joy. And as I was in a muse about this thing, that scrip-

[10] *Ibid.*, par. 206.

ture came in upon me, "Mercy rejoiceth against judgement."[11]

This does not mean the complete cessation of struggle. The disturbing texts recur, but Bunyan now has courage to look them in the face, and they no longer frighten or master him. In quaint but pungent words he states a deep-lying psychological truth regarding the resolution of conflict through its confrontation:

I began to take some measure of encouragement, to come close to them to read them, and consider them, and to weigh their scope and tendency. The which when I began to do, I found their visage changed: for they looked not so grimly as before I thought they did. . . .

And now remained only the hinder part of the tempest, for the thunder was gone beyond me, only some drops did still remain, that now and then would fall upon me. . . . Now did my chains fall off my legs indeed; I was loosed from mine afflictions and irons; my temptations also fled away; so that from that time those dreadful scriptures of God left off to trouble me. Now went I also home rejoicing, for the grace and love of God.[12]

Bunyan is not careful as to his chronology, but from what he says it is possible to deduce that these periods of acute disturbance lasted until he was about twenty-five. Two years later he felt the call to preach. During the early years of his ministry he had periods of great discouragement and nervous exhaustion, but also a strong sense of divine guidance. He had enough iron in

[11] *Ibid.*, par. 214.
[12] *Ibid.*, pars. 223-24, 229, 231.

his soul so that when he was arrested five years later for disobeying the Conventicle Act, he went to prison rather than agree to stop preaching. There he had been for five years when he wrote *Grace Abounding*.

The sequel must be added to round out the tale. After spending twelve years of his best years in prison, he was released in 1672 at the age of forty-four. He was chosen pastor of a nonconformist church in Bedford, with twenty-five or thirty churches under his supervision, and proved himself a capable executive. He had so much authority among the Baptists that he was popularly called Bishop Bunyan.

During a second imprisonment, in 1675, he wrote *Pilgrim's Progress*, which was published in 1678. The years following his final release were given to preaching and writing. When he died in 1688, he left about sixty different published works, most of them tracts and sermons, but among them the immortal hymn of which the first stanza reads:

> He who would valiant be
> 'Gainst all disaster,
> Let him in constancy
> Follow the Master.
> There's no discouragement
> Shall make him once relent
> His first avowed intent
> To be a pilgrim.

When you next sing that hymn, let me adjure you to think not only of valiant John Bunyan in Bedford Jail writing *Pilgrim's Progress* but of tormented, obsessed, victorious John Bunyan struggling to overcome by God's abounding grace the darkness within his soul.

We turn now to some contemporary persons who have been good enough to write out their "case history" at my request. All of these are persons with whom I became acquainted through the correspondence elicited by the article "If I Make My Bed in Hell." All have come through periods of acute depression and nervous exhaustion to what is, if not complete recovery, at least sufficient mastery for working effectiveness. All are basically Christian in their outlook and were aided in their recovery by Christian faith. Their statements may serve not only to give contemporaneity to our analysis but to indicate something of the road that leads out of darkness.

Naturally such intimate statements must be anonymous. For convenience in reference we shall call these correspondents Miss R, Mrs. L, Mr. D, and Miss N.

III

The first story is that of a well-adjusted, very capable high school teacher in her forties. This is what she says:

That I am at present actively engaged in the profession to which I have devoted my life since graduation from college, is a daily source of wonder to me. In truth, the "age of miracles" has not passed. The events of the last seven and a half years bear witness to this fact. During that period I passed through "deep waters" which threatened permanently to engulf me. I owe my present good health and splendid position to the love and mercy of God, for to him belongs the credit for my victory in the battle for health. Not of my own strength could I have ever surmounted the difficulties which befell me within the past decade.

In the fall of 1936 I suffered a serious nervous breakdown, which forced me to give up my teaching position for a period of two whole years. The illness took the form of a depression which lasted over a year. Four months of this time were spent in a private sanitarium, where some benefit was derived. The outlook seemed black indeed, and I despaired of ever regaining my health and being able to teach again. During this time I prayed constantly for help, but it seemed of no avail. Instead of prayer's bringing comfort, it brought me pain. I felt that I had forever forfeited the right to God's mercy, so deep was the burden of guilt and self-condemnation upon my soul. From early childhood I had been reared in the Christian faith, and had been a member of the Church, where I had been taught the efficacy of prayer.

During the second year of my absence from my work I recovered sufficiently to be able to enroll for a light program at a college, and later to do some part-time teaching. This proved to be a godsend, for hope and confidence in the possibility of a return to my work resulted. Thus, in the fall of 1938, I returned to my former position. Friends were exceedingly kind and understanding, welcoming me back as if nothing unusual had occurred. In a few days I felt as if I had never left my work. Three very happy and, I hope, successful teaching years passed. I enjoyed my work more than I had before my illness. My faith in God had been greatly strengthened by his wonderful gift of restored health, and I felt that I had conquered the world!

Let us interrupt the story for a comment or two. One finds here, as one does not in the accounts from earlier days, a conscious recognition of the therapeutic value of work. Also, there is a more humane attitude toward mental illness on the part of friends and co-workers. We have moved a few steps forward in this respect, though there is plenty of distance yet to go. But Miss R's spiritual desolation and self-condemnation are typical of the dark night. So is the apparent recovery, to be followed by relapse.

But alas for human pride! In the summer of 1941, at the close of these three happy years, I underwent a thyroidectomy. The operation was successful, but the nervous system was weakened by the shock. Just before the school term opened, my teaching assignment was changed, some new work being given me. The old enemies of fear and worry attacked me, and depression resulted. I attempted to teach that fall, but I was forced to give up at the conclusion of the first week. I returned to my home to fight my battle against "nerves."

If ever a human being was discouraged, it was I. Such utter misery and depression of soul overtook me that death would have been a welcome release. All of this time I had continued to pray for strength and guidance, but again I experienced no relief from the strain and tension. Although praying seemed to aggravate my emotional instability, yet I could not give it up, for it seemed my only hope.

It was at this period that a consulting psychologist, who had known me in previous years, did her best to give me back my faith in God (which I had all but lost) and in my future. She was most anxious that I return to my work. Upon her advice, strongly seconded by a doctor of medicine, I returned to my former position on a half-time basis. I had by no means recovered my full strength, but it seemed the only solution.

And so it proved. My psychologist friend had impressed upon me the truth of divine guidance in human affairs, being sure that if I made the effort to teach again, strength would be given to meet the need. Upon this principle I acted, and I was not disappointed.

The first month proved to be a daily battle to keep going. At times it seemed that I just couldn't continue my work, for it was an uphill fight. But God did not fail me, for he helped me wonderfully through my friends during that period. Once again, people were kind and considerate as before.

During these weeks I seemed to have been led to read just the right books. In this way I read Dr. E. Stanley Jones's *Is the Kingdom of God Realism?* and Alice Bretz's *I Begin Again* (a most unusual book of courage). Two other books which were also illuminating at this time were *The Rediscovery of Man* by Dr. Henry C. Link, and Peale and Blanton's *Faith Is the Answer.* To all of these authors I owe a great debt of gratitude for their most timely help in a period of crisis.

The combined therapy of useful work, understanding friends, the aid of a Christian psychologist, and discerning books was very helpful. The decisive element in her renewal came from a discovery—simple yet profound —which released the tensions and gave strength to fight. She continues:

During this period I made a discovery which was overwhelming in its effect upon me. For the first time I saw the relations between the physical, mental, and spiritual aspects of my illness. I learned that other people had suffered as I, and had triumphed! One was not altogether condemned because of failure to find spiritual victory, and there was a way out of the dilemma. For the first time I was able to forgive myself.

In three months I was back to normal; my work at school

had greatly improved, and life was beautiful and joyous once more. One can scarcely describe the joy one experiences when a soul-crushing burden of despair is finally lifted by a merciful God. The "turning point" in my recovery came when I ceased regretting the past, ceased pitying myself, and asked only for God and his presence and his power in my life. I know what it means to "hunger and thirst after righteousness" and then to experience the joy of being filled. During the past two years of full-time teaching the promise contained in Matthew 6:33 has been wonderfully fulfilled in my life. I look with hope to the future.

IV

The scene shifts now to Mrs. L, a woman physician happily married to an electrical engineer, with three normal children. She has culture, wide interests, religious sensitivity, and outwardly all that is required for a right adjustment to life. Yet only recently has she emerged from years of inward darkness. This is her story:

For years I lived under the shadow of severe depressions. Fatigue, insomnia, or an emotional conflict—and I dropped without warning into an abyss where I ceased to be a thinking, loving person. Exhausted, crying, I found small household tasks great burdens, although years of discipline taught me to finish up my dishes or whatever else before I crawled into bed. I could not bear to talk to people, or to have them see me reduced to protoplasm. My usual enjoyments had no appeal. Sleep—as oblivion and as healer—was all I craved. And nervous tension banished sleep. Occasionally large doses of sedative helped. I had steadfastly to resist the temptation to make certain of oblivion by morphine; I thank God that there I succeeded. My husband's efforts to reason me out of this state simply widened the chasm I felt between all the world and me.

I tried to pray but without avail. The God I trusted I could not find in my extremity. Why?

Between these episodes I lived a fairly normal life, making some contribution, I trust, to my family and community. But I knew I must somehow attain stability if I were to help build the Kingdom of God. Was there no one who understood both the ways of the mind and of the soul?

My search brought me finally to a doctor who did. After a thorough physical examination he showed me this train of circumstances: an inferiority complex persisting in spite of professional training; life with an unusually gifted person whom I all but worshiped; conflict between my loving pride in my husband's achievements and the lack of achievement I felt; lack of fulfillment interpreted as fatigue, which I attempted to overcome by further limiting my outlets and adding to the frustration.

The doctor's injunction was essentially that of Jesus long ago: "Launch out into the deep." Back I must go into my profession for a sense of fulfillment; carry on a normal social life; rest a reasonable amount, then disregard any remaining fatigue.

And why could I not find God during my mood swings? They represented domination of my brain by the thalamus, center of emotions. The cerebrum, with which I normally thought and prayed, was dethroned by it. This unruly member I must snub—by a change of scene, like an evening at the library with a good medical book. I must cease to fear its tyranny and say to myself, "This is only a mood swing; it will pass." Ultimately the mood swings would become less in frequency and amplitude.

So it has been. The sense of contributing to the community through my loved profession, part-time, has given me new relish for domestic duties, each enhancing the other. Insomnia and tension have shrunk amazingly. Fulfillment is undermining the inferiority which is a denial of God's gifts.

Wisely, my counselor emphasized the ups and downs in any program. The tendency to emotional upheavals is not overcome in a year. It requires patience for my family and me, until new habits can be built. But now we live in hope. For with this help in clearing away the underbrush, I believe that daily I can make straight in the desert of my own life a highway for my God.

The situation here is different from any of the other cases traced, though the phenomena of depression, insomnia, fatigue, withdrawal, and spiritual inadequacy are true to type. The root of the trouble was found, not in any overt domestic or religious disharmony, but in an unconscious overshadowing within the home, and even more, I suspect, in an unresolved conflict between the demands of domesticity and professional life.

Obviously, Mrs. L could not give up her home. But could she have solved the problem by concentrating resolutely on her home to the exclusion of a career? I doubt it. It is futile to quote glibly, "Woman's sphere is the home," and disregard the fact that when a woman is equipped to serve both in her home and in her profession, both avenues must have expression. Mrs. L's inability to find strength in God in spite of her warmly religious nature illustrates the frequency with which family and vocational situations lift their heads in the midst of all manner of religious problems.

V

The third testimony is from a man, who on account of ill health and uncertainty about himself has not married, but who by the help of a combination of psychiatry and religion has found the way out of depression to usefulness and a high degree of mastery. This is his story:

My mother died when I was thirteen; then followed three years of loneliness and overwork as my father and I did the work in the house and on the farm and I walked two miles and a half to school. My father was very strict with me, and I did not think then that he had any understanding of me or cared that my lot was so hard.

The onset of depressions came when I was sixteen. What had happened to me I did not know. I only knew, from the first, that my mental powers and the ability to do my school work that had always been so easy were impaired. I "stood alone and the darkness hemmed me in and there was no one to deliver me." Various doctors, the best general practitioners in the state, ascribed my illness to this and that physical cause. There were several minor operations. A change of climate was recommended for a supposedly virulent form of malaria and I lived in the West for six years.

The predominating feeling through all of this was that I was insane. I wanted to be put away in an institution where nobody could see me. I started college, but gave it up after a year. After that I lived at home but on account of my illness did nothing but occasional jobs.

During this time I felt baffled that religion did not help me more. My people were staunch church members and I had loved to go to church and admired Christian people all my life. I had been able to get from my religion in my health problem, however, solace but not victory.

Yet it was from the combined assistance of psychiatry and religion that Mr. D found release, after having "suffered many things of many physicians." A psychiatrist of broad culture and deep insight convinced him both of the necessity and the possibility of a drastic change in personality. Assumption of responsibility for regular, though limited, work was the first step. But deeper changes must be wrought.

Unfortunately, the mere knowledge of this did not summon the necessary inner resources for changes in my life. I felt instinctively that the needed courage and strength would have to come from a Power outside myself.

During that next summer I found a newness of faith that I had not known. My chief venture in the search of the Scriptures was a reading of all the epistles of St. Paul and the marking and study of all passages that admonished the abandonment of fear. One immediate reward in the realm of the spiritual that year was genuine and complete forgiveness of my father for his domineering restrictions on me. I came to see that he was only safeguarding my morals as he thought necessary. He did not know, nor had he had the opportunity to know, what he was doing to my emotional life.

It is significant that the ability to forgive his father, which came as the direct result of the message of divine forgiveness with which Paul's letters are filled, lifted the weight of a long-imbedded sense of injury. This was undoubtedly an important factor in making further achievement possible. Mr. D then returned to college, from which he had been out ten years, and graduated as valedictorian of his class. The story continues:

My spiritual life reached a new high point the next year in my having the opportunity to hear and meet Dr. E. Stanley Jones. He made me know that he knew what fear was and how to overcome it as he spoke on "The Conquest of Fear." He has continued to sound certain great themes in his ministry that have been very helpful to me. Among these I have found three that have been most beneficial: (1) Do not put your struggles on the basis of your will to overcome: "Let go. Let God." (2) The Christian way is the natural way. One finds true satisfaction in following Christ, and one will break himself if he breaks the laws of the Kingdom. (3) You must not "waste your pains" as the pagans did, in Jeremiah 51:58 (Moffatt); you must build something fine into your life from your sufferings.

At present I am doing social work with underprivileged children, many of whom have emotional problems. I find satisfactions and a large degree of fulfillment in my work. I cannot claim that I have no tendency to depression but I have met several periods of threatened depression with much less fear than formerly, and each time I have been able to go ahead with my daily work. In some measure I am able to say with Matthew Arnold:

> Tasks in hours of insight willed
> Can be through hours of gloom fulfilled.

The hymns "Just as I Am" and "When I Survey the Wondrous Cross" have come to mean a great deal to me. To come to Christ and to know that he has suffered and understands are saving experiences.

The victory recorded here, as in most cases of the conquest of depression, is not cataclysmic change but gradual upturn in the power to face life with courage, determination, and usefulness. With such an outcome one does not have to "waste his pains"!

VI

Our last statement is from a professional church worker, more mystical in temperament than our other contemporary cases and more articulate in describing her religious struggles and victories. Miss N's story, though in a modern setting, runs closer to the classic experience of the dark night:

What was my state of mind in this "black night of the soul"?

There was ever and again the wish to be dead. If I could just cease to exist! But that was the rub. I believed that dying did not end it all. I felt a resentment that it did not. It seems ridiculous now, but I had thought out the exact nonmessy method by which I could take my own life with the least trouble to others. And yet, I knew I would never do it, at least not while Mother and Dad lived. A sense of family loyalty forbade that, even if a fear of the future life, or cowardice, had not.

There was also a fear of insanity. Sometimes I thought maybe I *was* insane. It is a peculiarly distressful thing to go about your work acting like any other human being but knowing within yourself that you really aren't normal. You are seething within in fear of your sanity, eager to be done with life; and as you talk with folks you carry on a stream of thought all your own and wonder what those people would think if they knew what kind of a person they were talking to.

Toward those few good people who gave me their utmost in precious friendship I would cry out at times wishing to God that they had been spared the knowledge of me, for I was so sure that in the end I could bring them only pain. And in the same breath I cried to them not to let me go, to hold me fast to them; for I knew that without them I could not endure myself, I would be lost indeed.

Note here not only the common tendency to fear insanity and to play with the idea of suicide, but an overwhelming sense of inferiority which led her at the same time to shrink from her friends and to cling to them. With such inner conflict, spiritual chaos was inevitable. The story continues:

I hungered to know God, to have a fellowship with him. But it seemed that I could know him only through the experiences of others, only through hearsay. Internally I lived in hell though I walked the earth.

But I no longer live in hell. I still walk the earth, but I live in heaven. How did I get there?

With the coming of a new pastor and his wife my trouble was brought to a climax. The impact of his sermons, their own lives, and their love toward me were such that the self I wanted to be came into sharp conflict with the self that I knew I was. I went to the hospital with a "nervous breakdown." The Potter had to shatter his vessel before he could remold it. But how grateful I am that he considered it worthy material for remolding.

The friends, helpful though they were, were apparently not wise enough to make sure that the sufferer's deliverance was a personal transaction between her and God.

In my pastor's home one day soon after my return I was committed to God. I'm sorry, but I have to put it that way. Had I broken through my reserve and spoken aloud and given myself, instead of letting another do it for me, I think much delay and grief would have been avoided. And yet I can't be sure. I only know I became aware that my commitment was not entire. My friends still had first place in my life. My depression was lightened, but swift terrible periods of blackness would overwhelm me still. But these periods diminished as I came into increasing fellowship with God. Every new experience of the love, or patience, or forgiveness of my two friends led me to exclaim, "Why, God must be like that —only more so!" And I wanted to know him even as my friends knew him.

Without the help of such friendship it is doubtful whether Miss N would have recovered. But, as has happened repeatedly in similar counselings, moralistic advice almost thwarted the value of such loving understanding:

I was finding, too, great help in the sermons of my pastor. He was definitely trying to help me, both in and out of the pulpit. And oh, the heartaches that involved! It was only because I *knew* they loved me and wanted to help me that I was able to swallow the fact that they were forever "trying to teach me something."

The beloved pastor moved to another parish. Now came the question as to whether Miss N's new-found spiritual strength could stand alone with the help of God. It met the test and she found herself surrounded by the presence of God, within which earthly separations were transcended. From the reading of the Bible came great new insights. An experience is recorded which may seem meaningless or abnormal to some readers, but the earlier mystics would have responded to it as authentic. In any case, it was justified by its fruits.

Another experience had come previously. It has been my stay in many difficult moments since, and it gave me a great sense of assurance of God's care for me. I was returning from my first venture into a work experience following my illness. I was dreading separation from my friends, knowing that when I was alone I would be seized with despair over myself, that all the old torments would come swarming in upon me. But I went on into my home. Finally I went into my own room, and I had scarcely entered until I felt myself almost visibly surrounded by that which was so real it seemed to have weight; I felt an impulse to reach my hand out to take hold of it. A strange sense of peace came to me, an abeyance of thought almost; a sense of awe and wonderment filled me, and I knew that that which surrounded me was God's love and God's power *refusing to let me be discouraged with myself.*

The story concludes with a number of incidents which are at the same time cause and evidence of spiritual conquest of her earlier trouble:

There was the boost which came from being "on the job" again; a week at a Sunday school camp in a working capacity; and the attendance upon a "Camp Farthest Out," out of which have grown some most liberating and enlightening experiences. There was the reading of Glenn Clark's *I Will Lift Up Mine Eyes,* which I believe God sent for my time of need. Some beautiful new experiences have come this past winter and spring. So far I've kept these a secret between God and me; and that, I find, has been a powerful factor in bringing me that sense of nearness and companionship with God which makes it easy to accord him first place in my life and thoughts.

Had I been free to take on some work of the kind I loved in our church here, I think I would have pulled out of this trouble much sooner. I've had a terrible time accommodating myself to the situation here, for which I am partly responsible because of my own failure. To forgive myself for that failure; not to feel envy or bitterness toward those who have carried on in the job I preferred; to accept God's discipline and find in it his love and my own freedom, was all a part of the struggle into "light." But I'd go through it all again, if need be, for the glory that has come to me because I have found him who is indeed the Light of Life.

This outcome is what St. John of the Cross would have called "the ascent of Mt. Carmel" to the vision of God's glory. Let one compare it with the mood of the opening paragraphs of Miss N's story and he can see what Jesus meant when he said, "Thy faith hath made thee whole."

Chapter IV

Some Theological Implications

WE HAVE UNCOVERED THE PROBLEM OF THE DARK night of the soul and by citations of various cases, ancient and modern, have seen how it assails and cripples personality. Doubtless some readers by now are saying, "That's only a nervous breakdown. Let's move on. How do you get over it?"

That the dark night is a form of the multiform psychic disturbance popularly called a nervous breakdown is to be admitted.[1] One may be in it without reaching the state of nervous collapse which incapacitates one for work or normal social relations, but it moves in that direction. In the more extreme forms it may lead to insanity or suicide—the victim often fears this outcome —but usually it does not. Its distinguishing characteristic is a deep depression from which the sufferer, however sincere his religious experience, feels himself unable

---

[1] The most satisfactory discussion of the religious significance of such neurotic disturbance is by a Danish physician, Dr. Hans Jacob Schou, in his *Religion and Morbid Mental States.* Originally appearing in Denmark in 1924 as lectures to young theological students, it was published in English in 1926 by the Century Co. (London: Methuen and Co.). The literature on this subject is appallingly meager.

to emerge, and before which the grace of God seems unavailable.

Though the reader might like to move straightway to further analysis of its causes and cure (and no one can prevent him from skipping this section if he wants to!), it is impossible to move on so quickly and be on safe ground. The dark night is so complex and baffling a phenomenon that it must be understood in the wider context of God's relation to his world.

I

It is the Christian faith that a personal God—holy, righteous, and loving—has created men in his own spiritual image. He has made us for fellowship with himself and for the attainment of high ends in service to one another. He has placed us in a physical universe of remarkable orderliness, utility, and beauty, and has so constituted this material order, including our bodies, that when rightly adjusted and used it provides all that is needed for our physical well-being. He has made us free spirits capable of moral choices, and he has limited his own freedom to manipulate events at will by giving to us all the freedom we need for responsible and happy living. He has placed us in an extremely complex system of social relations, so that our lives inevitably depend upon and influence other lives for good or evil. This physical and social framework in which our lives are set both imposes limitations to our action and offers high opportunities.

Within this setting all men are called to do the will of God. This is stated by Jesus in the injunction to "seek first the kingdom of God, and his righteousness." Though there is not full agreement as to the precise forms of action required by this ideal of the Kingdom, its requirements as set forth by Jesus are, in general outlines, unmistakable. To do the will of God and work with him for the coming of his Kingdom demands of us self-giving love, humility, inward purity, childlike trust, courageous and resolute action to bring to all men "the abundant life." To engage willfully in acts or to acquiesce in attitudes contrary to this goal is sin.

Sin always involves volition, whether in acting or refraining from action. Both in our bodies and in our spirits there are other derangements, maladjustments, aberrations from what ought to be, which are not ordinarily willed by us, and which constitute one form or another of physical or mental illness.

Is the dark night of the soul a form of sin, of which we must repent and look to God for cleansing? Or is it a disease, a limitation to be corrected by discovery of causes and alteration of circumstances?

Clearly, it makes a difference. If it is sin, the appropriate mood is recognition of guilt and repentance; and the way to moral regeneration is the new life that comes to the penitent sinner through God's forgiving grace. If it is sickness, whether physical or mental, the sufferer needs a competent doctor and the rectification of whatever factors are causing the maladjustment. Both one's judgment of himself and the way others judge him— and, in consequence, the therapy—are greatly dependent on the answer given to this question.

The tendency to regard such spiritual darkness as

sinful has long held sway in Christian thought. In the medieval church it was one of the seven deadly sins— the sin of "accidie." [2] To translate *acedia* or *accidie* simply as "sloth" is to miss the overtones of spiritual torpor, disquiet, gloom, and futility which accidie connotes. It meant the spiritual sluggishness which cuts the nerve of positive effort for good and plunges one into sullen inactivity. Dante calls it "a foul and lazy mist within," and has its victims mired in the fifth circle of Hell as a consequence of their wrathfulness upon earth. Of their plight he says:

> Fixed in the slime they say: "Sullen were we
> In the sweet air that's gladdened by the sun,
> Having within our hearts the smoke of sloth;
> Now we are sullen in the swarthy mire."
> This hymn they gurgle in their throats, because
> With perfect words they cannot utter it. [3]

In *Il Purgatorio,* where accidie is purged away, Dante describes its negative character in a swift, deft stroke:

> The love of good, come short
> Of what it should effect, is here restored. [4]

Chaucer in *The Canterbury Tales* makes the Parson

[2] Pronounced ak'sid-ie. It should be made clear that my identification of accidie with the dark night does not follow medieval thought. Accidie was a sin to be shunned; the dark night, according to St. John of the Cross, was a purgative experience to be coveted as leading the chosen soul to God. Psychologically, the phenomena seem to me indistinguishable. The difference lies not in the form of the experience but in the interpretation placed upon it and, consequently, in its effects.

[3] *The Divine Comedy* (tr. Johnson; Yale, 1915), *Inferno,* Canto VII, ll. 121-26.

[4] *Ibid., Purgatorio,* Canto XVII, ll. 85 f.

denounce "the rotten-hearted sin of accidie," and in quaint but graphic Old English says that the person who commits it does everything "with annoy, and with rawness, slackness, and excusation." [5] St. Ignatius of Loyola is not quite so forthright, but in his *Spiritual Exercises* he writes vividly of spiritual desolation as "darkness and confusion of soul, attraction towards base and earthly objects, disquietude caused by various agitations and temptations which make the soul distrustful, without hope and love, so that it finds itself altogether slothful, tepid, sad, and, as it were, separated from its Creator and Lord." Such a state, to the good Catholic, could be nothing short of sinful.[6]

In religious circles still, it is the usual thing to regard darkness of spirit as sin. Are we not bidden to have faith in God, and is not such darkness essentially a denial of faith? Must we not be grateful to God for his gifts, and is not despondency a form of thanklessness? Also, on the human plane, is it not our duty to spread cheer, and is not gloom a sin against our neighbor? There is often also a lurking judgment, like the suspicion of Job's friends, that if the victim had not sinned somewhere he would not have got himself into this state.

Outside of religious circles, and to some extent within them where a scientific study of human personality has gained foothold, the tendency, on the other hand, is to regard depression as a form of mental illness. This leads to objectivity of analysis and charity of judgment,

---

[5] "The Parson's Tale," pars. 53, 55.
[6] "Rules for the Discernment of Spirits," rule 4.

and often to wholesome effort to discover and remedy the causes. So far, so good.

But what of the Christian idea that evil moods and acts require repentance and surrender of the self to God? From the point of view of psychiatry, a sense of guilt, far from being a means of deliverance by the channel of God's forgiving grace, is itself usually a symptom of neurotic personality. Instead of surrendering to God, one is commonly enjoined to get rid of cramping inhibitions and express one's self. Such self-expression may range from sexual indulgence to the highest artistic creativity. It may be linked with an incentive to altruistic service in an attempt to overcome introversion, and often takes the form of enlarging the range of the sufferer's interests and increasing his self-confidence.

But this is still self-expression, not self-surrender or self-denial. It runs so counter to basic Christian insights that religious people are often suspicious of psychotherapy, and brand it as "Freudian" without knowing much about Freud. Granted that this suspicion is usually mixed with misunderstanding, the case is as broad as it is long, for not many psychiatrists understand much about religion. Thus the chasm widens from both sides, and the patient—already confused—is lost in still greater confusion.

It is the main contention of this book that what we are dealing with is *both* a sin and a disease. Short of this recognition I doubt whether it is possible to have a right therapy based on a right understanding. To the extent that depression is subject to control by the will, one sins to remain in it. Short of complete insanity there are always areas of freedom left, and in these areas the sufferer is morally responsible. Yet by its very nature normal volition is curtailed, and to the extent that freedom is limited one becomes, not a sinner to be judged, but a sick person to be healed.

The extreme complexity and difficulty of the problem arises from the fact that the phenomenon we are discussing lies just at the borderline of freedom, and looks in both directions. Therefore it cannot be dealt with by procedures applicable either to overt sin or to clearly recognizable disease. To condemn it as sin and urge repentance is often to accentuate rather than lighten the sufferer's misery. He knows he is a sinner and too often really has a "guilt psychosis" which exaggerates his self-condemnation. It is not enough simply to hold out the hope of divine forgiveness, for if he is a sensitive Christian he has doubtless already prayed many times for forgiveness without apparent result. On the other hand, to overlook the fact of sin and find the causes of the malady only in environmental, social, physiological, and psychic maladjustments is greatly to oversimplify the human situation. As we shall see in ensuing chapters, when all has been done that can be done to rectify bad conditions, the ultimate release comes only by a religious solution.

II

A second deep theological question which impinges on our problem is what is meant by "the will of God." Does God will everything to happen as it does? In the presence of every evil thing should one say, "This is the will of God"? No matter what disaster befalls one's self or one's loved ones, is it the Christian attitude to say, "Let us accept it without murmuring as God's mysterious providence"?

Christian theology has never been very consistent at this point. Even where predestination has not been as explicit as in Calvinism, the main stream both of church doctrine and of naïve Christian assumption has hesitated to question the governance of God in the tragedies of life. Multitudes of people are able to accept the most bitter suffering with resignation because they say, "It was to be. God knows best." The Garden prayer, "Nevertheless not my will, but thine, be done," says something so true to the heart of Christian experience that it has ever since been a call to faith and hope in the midst of the mysteries of pain.

Certainly no Christian without arrant presumption and untruth could deny God's presence in the human struggle and the need of *accepting* as well as of *doing* his will. But, when looked at from the other side, what the acceptance of everything as God's will comes out at is perilously near the conclusion that whatever is, is right. And can we possibly suppose that everything that happens *is* God's will? The crippling and starving of little children, the bombing of helpless civilians, the sacrifice of millions of young men in their best years, the ravages of disease, the constant cutting off of life prematurely and violently, even apart from the obscene destructiveness of war—can these things be willed by God? And what of brilliant minds, not cut off mercifully by death, but condemned to the living death of hopeless insanity? To say that all this is God's will is to assume, in the graphic words of John Stuart Mill, "that God does every day things which men are hanged for doing."

It is the basic Christian necessity both to affirm and not to affirm God's causal activity in the disasters of life that makes the problem of evil such a deep-rooted and interminable question. Nobody can claim to have solved it fully. The most satisfactory answer is to say that God *permits* what he does not *will,* and that whatever happens, he wills that we make good come out of evil.

The question of why God permits evil events to happen cannot be answered apart from the general structure of Christian thought which was outlined at the beginning of this chapter. We live in an orderly physical universe; our lives are woven together in an intricate system of social relations; and within this setting we have been endowed by God with the supreme gift of moral freedom. If we are to have freedom to act in a dependable world, God cannot set aside at our request either the physical regularities or social connections within which our lives are placed. This "order of creation" is such an incalculable blessing that no thoughtful person would want it set aside if we could have it so. But within this order our freedom is at many points restricted, and both man's will and God's are sometimes thwarted. Our challenge is to use our freedom in God's world for his ends, doing what we can to change evil situations, enduring what we must.

The bearing of this on our problem is clear, though the depth of the difficulty has been obscured by the view that though *events* might be contrary to God's will, our *attitudes* need never be. The usual Christian assumption is that though there are evil situations—really evil ones before which neither God nor man can be complacent—no man need be defeated by them in his own soul.

The phenomenon of the dark night, if the facts are as we have stated them, is a direct challenge both to the assumption that whatever happens is God's will and that spiritual victory is always available. I, for one, cannot believe that God directly wills the misery described in the preceding chapters. Though men *have* been led through it to sainthood, the loss among the many who have not is incalculable. And if spiritual victory were immediately available, the "night" would not be dark.

III

This leads to the question so central to the thought of St. John of the Cross, that of divine purgation. Granted that God does not arbitrarily send the misery of the dark night, may it not still be his holy purpose through it to purge the sufferer of dross and fit him for great tasks?

This is what the greater mystics and saints have always believed. Though accidie was sin, the dark night led upward. Because the light of the mount of vision lay beyond it, the night, in retrospect, was rejoiced in as God's precious gift. St. John of the Cross warns against the danger of confusing such purgation with "melancholy or some other imperfection with respect to sense or to spirit." [7] The soul whom God is leading "by a most lofty path of dark contemplation and aridity, wherein it seems to be lost," will, he says, meet one who will speak to it like Job's comforters and say that it is suffering from melancholy or low spirits, or morbidity of temperament, or that it may have some hidden sin, and that for this reason God has forsaken it. St. John thought it essential for confessors to see that of joys and afflictions, hopes and griefs, some proceed from the spirit of perfection and others from imperfection.

As previously suggested, I do not believe that so simple a distinction can be drawn. St. John of the Cross was basically right, as against "Job's comforters," in holding that the roots of the dark night may lie in religious devotion rather than hidden sin. But as may be seen by glancing back at the cases surveyed in the previous chapter, there is not one of the six who did not, while the depression was deepest, feel overmastered by destructive forces. All could have surrendered and ended their days in insanity or hopeless futility. Yet all triumphed, by God's help, to become useful and victorious servants of God. Was their darkness of spirit the sin of accidie, or was it God's gift?

No answer is possible without the bringing together of the divine and human factors in the situation. Among many uncertainties we can be sure that God has ordained and maintains causal sequences in psychic as in

[7] *The Ascent of Mount Carmel*, Prologue, par. 4.

physical matters, that he desires no one to be futile or needlessly unhappy, that he seeks to bring all men to the light of his presence and his service. Such attainment of power as may follow the dark night is no human achievement, but God's gift. Yet, from our side, conditions must be met. It is as we conform to his established ways, rest in his strength, respond to his leading with such feeble will power as we have, that more power is given and the soul is refined. In retrospect, the painful journey of the dark night may rightly be interpreted by St. John of the Cross, or by any modern sufferer, as God's purgation for great ends. But it becomes so only as, while one is passing through it, one does all that one can to let the light of God shine through the darkness.

IV

A closely related theological issue which has to be faced is that of the limits and possibilities of prayer. Unanswered prayer is one of the most common characteristics of the dark night, and one of the most poignant sources of misery. If we could simply pray and find ourselves strong again, the problem would be nonexistent.

There has been misunderstanding both of the deeper causes of emotional insecurity and of the way in which God works to lift its burden. It is now generally assumed that if one has a broken back he will not "arise and walk" immediately, but that if one has a broken spirit all that is needed to set it right is prayer and confidence in God's healing power. That God heals in both cases when the conditions of his physical and spiritual order are met is a basic tenet of Christian faith. But that a miracle is not to be expected in the first instance and can be expected in the second is an error productive of much unnecessary suffering.

Depression or despair is a form of acute nervous disturbance. When nerves are upset the cause lies in emotional conflict, in some irritation of the autonomic nervous system of the body, or, as frequently happens, in both, with a vicious circle in which each factor is made worse by the other. Though prayer is the primary source of emotional stability, it is a kind of blasphemy to suppose that prayer, unaided by an understanding of the causes of distress or by an attempt to remedy them, will do all that God requires.

Often the first service a counselor needs to render is to help a sufferer, whose own perspective is too clouded to see clearly, to discover what has caused his acute unhappiness. Sometimes the cause lies mainly in evil attitudes, such as anger, resentment, jealousy, sensuality, pride, egoism, or whatever is commonly meant by sin. Sometimes it is in fear, anxiety, inferiority, a fundamental distrust of oneself which is reflected in distrust of the world and a feeling of the meaninglessness of life. Sometimes these attitudes have been caused chiefly by objective factors, such as a turn of events that precipitates bitter disappointment, loss of economic security, bereavement, or the enforced partings and uncertainties of war.

Sometimes these circumstances are objectively of great seriousness; again, though trifling, they are magnified in imagination. Sometimes such causes of distress break upon the individual with sudden shock to shatter his world, while frequently they are to be found in such persistent social sores as race and class antagonisms, poverty, drudgery, unemployment, vocational maladjustments, and domestic tensions. As was suggested in our first chapter, sometimes the primary sources of despair lie neither in evil attitudes nor in social forces but in certain peculiarly disturbing bodily conditions.

We shall canvass these causes more fully in later chapters. They bear directly on the matter of prayer; for though prayer can do much to eliminate them, particularly where personal attitudes are the main factor, it cannot do everything. We ought not to expect it to. Some conditions can be changed greatly through prayer, others little or not at all. Even Jesus had to pray in the Garden, "My Father, if it be possible . . ." [8]

It is clear that, since depression can have so many different sources, no uniform treatment is applicable to all. It is true that in *any* condition prayer and faith are better than rebellion and distrust, and there is no situation, however dark, in which God does not seek to impart strength. It is not true that by faith alone every broken spirit can be healed. God works with man to lift and heal, but only through the eradication of barriers in our total psychophysical existence can his Spirit have an unhindered channel. Recognition of the limits as well as the possibilities of prayer leads to release from the bitterness of expectations unfulfilled, but also to clearer understanding and more potent faith as we seek to work with God by meeting his conditions.

[8] Matt. 26:39.

V

A moot but crucial question relating to our theme is the problem of perfectionism. The word has several meanings, though all suggest disparity of some sort between the ideal and the actual.

To the psychologist, one of the commonest forms of psychic disturbance is that caused by the disrupting inner conflict that appears when one refuses to accept one's limitations, and yearns to be or to do what is beyond the possibility of attainment. Or in a less serious form, perfectionism means nervous fussiness, an unreasonable insistence on getting every detail in the object of attention exactly right to the neglect of more important matters. In religious diction, Christian perfection has sometimes connoted a doctrine of entire sanctification, a state of holiness imparted by the Holy Spirit after conversion and eagerly sought as a mark of God's favor. In more recent theological discussion, perfectionism is used to refer to the absoluteness of the ethics of Jesus and the assumption of the perfectionists (usually a derogatory epithet) that by trying hard enough they can do what the Christian ethic demands.

All of these meanings, disparate as they seem, have a central thrust bearing on our problem. They converge in the fact that, though one cannot live without ideals of some sort, unhappiness ensues when one realizes the gap between his ideal and its attainment. The gap may be at least partially closed by pulling the ideal down, as when one "stops trying to amount to anything." Or it may be obscured by the illusion of attainment, as in the holiness sects. But, for the Christian saint, the higher the ideal, the keener his awareness of his failure to reach it.

When a sensitive Christian knows that he ought to be happy and useful in God's service yet finds himself unhappy, futile, and unable to pass from what he is to what he ought to be, the dark night of the soul is upon him. All minor frustrations are magnified; yet all together they are a trifle compared with the overwhelming frustration of inability to meet what one believes that God demands. This is why self-reproach is so common among those who, to others, seem to have little to reproach themselves for.

Does God demand of us such perfection that our failure must lead to despair? On the one hand, there is the "Be ye perfect" of Jesus, and requirements in the Sermon on the Mount that call for nothing less. Jesus could meet them—but can we? No Christian, however saintly he appears to others, is flawless, and to assume one's own perfection is most unsaintly presumption. "If we say that we have no sin, we deceive ourselves, and the truth is not in us." [9] Are we commanded, then, to strive after perfection and doomed always to the frustration of defeat?

The way out lies along the route which Paul discovered and described with great vividness in his letter to the Romans. One can be so weighed down by his inability to do good as to feel chained to "the body of this death"; one can also say, "There is . . . now no condemnation to them that are in Christ Jesus. For the law of the Spirit of life in Christ Jesus made me free from

[9] I John 1:8.

the law of sin and of death." Millions have found victory by this route.

For the Christian there can be no blotting out of the disparity between ideal and actual. "Be ye therefore perfect, even as your Father which is in heaven is perfect" [10] is a continuing reminder of demands we shall never meet. Awareness of this tension is the spur that goads us out of the lethargy of complacency. But it need not overwhelm us, or drive us to despair. If one believes in the mercy as well as the judgment of God, one can leave with God's forgiving love one's shortcomings and press forward, empowered for better service in his Kingdom. Excessive self-condemnation in the Christian is distrust of God's everlasting mercy. If God is love, it is a kind of blasphemy to stagger along under a burden of despair.

VI

Finally, we need a clearer understanding of the sources of the faith by which to lay hold upon God's grace. Seeking to emphasize the divine initiative and leave no place for salvation by works, Luther and Calvin held that God imparts not only grace but faith. Reacting against the predestinarian implications of this view, modern religious thought has generally made faith a matter of will, the human precondition of receiving what God stands ready to impart. The truth lies in both views, not in either alone.

Whether in the older Protestant orthodoxy or the new, the assumption that faith as well as grace is the

[10] Matt. 5:48 (A.V.).

special gift of God not only leads logically to a doctrine of election but morally leads to despair when one feels bereft of it. But the paradox of the matter is that when, realizing his plight, one tries feverishly to lay hold upon God's grace, one is apt to find, instead of victory, only a worse nervous tension than before. Once more it is a kind of blasphemy to try to save ourselves by storming the battlements of heaven to get God to save us.

The way out, theologically and therapeutically, lies in the recognition that faith is both a gift and a task. Where one believes, as a Christian may, that in God we live and move and have our being, one has only to open the doors of his soul to discover that he rests always in God's all-encompassing love. When one believes that God has revealed himself with life-transforming clarity in Jesus Christ and through Christ has brought redemption to men, one does not need to strain with subjective activism to do for himself what Christ has done for us. When we believe that God bears in his heart the eternal tragedy of the world, we can believe that he bears our griefs and our transgressions. Yet, however gratefully we accept this gift of faith, acceptance does not mean passive acquiescence. It means the glad response of the soul to what God gives, and the taking upon oneself of the hard requirements of Christian discipleship.

The divine-human character of saving faith lies at the heart of the New Testament message. But it appears in the Old Testament as well, and many of the psalms are resonant with the note of divine assurance which is also a divine demand. In the eighty-fourth is a watch-word for any victim of the dark night of the soul:

"Passing through the valley of Weeping they make it a place of springs." [11]

How can they make of the vale of bitterness a place of living water? Look to the previous sentence for the key:

Blessed is the man whose strength is in thee;
In whose heart are the highways to Zion.

[11] Ps. 84:6.

Chapter V

The Shadow of Death

I

IN THE PREVIOUS CHAPTER WE CANVASSED SOME CON-
siderations bearing on our problem with reference to sin
and weakness, the will of God in evil events, purgation,
prayer and its answer, perfectionism, the gift of God's
grace for the lifting of the burden of spiritual heaviness.
Another question, both theological and personal, is of
such immediate relation not only to the dark night but
to our total human situation that it merits a chapter of
its own.

The victim of the dark night has a paradoxical, and
what must always seem to onlookers an irrational, attitude toward death. With part of his mind he wants des-
perately to die. It seems the only way out of a situation
so packed full of misery that death is eagerly coveted.
In the case histories previously recorded, one notes such
testimonies. "Such utter misery and depression of soul
overtook me that death would have been a welcome
release." "There was ever and again the wish to be
dead." We found Jeremiah longing for nonexistence,
and Job saying,

> . . . my soul chooseth strangling,
> And death rather than these my bones.

But this is only part of the story. The sufferer longs to die, but he also fears and dreads to die. The conflict is further intensified, though from a broader standpoint greatly aided in solution, by the fact that the temptation to self-destruction is resisted both by a biological impulse to live and by at least a residuum of ethical restraint. Though contemplation of suicide is one of the commonest features of the dark night, it seldom actually happens. The sufferer, in spite of himself, is mercifully restrained by fear of death, concern for family and friends, and by a seldom wholly obliterated belief that suicide is wrong. All these factors are clear in the first paragraph of Miss N's statement:

There was ever and again the wish to be dead. If I could just cease to exist! But that was the rub. I believed that dying did not end it all. I felt a resentment that it did not. . . . And yet, I knew I would never do it, at least not while Mother and Dad lived. A sense of family loyalty forbade that, even if a fear of the future life, or cowardice, had not.

Here is Hamlet's soliloquy in contemporary prose. Shakespeare showed penetrating understanding of this state of mind when he wrote:

> To die, to sleep;
> To sleep: perchance to dream: ay, there's the rub;
> For in that sleep of death what dreams may come . . .

It is common for the sufferer to be wretched from

his plight but still more wretched from his indecision "to be or not to be." We found Jeremiah crying out in the midst of his longing for escape, "Take me not away in thy longsuffering." The present is dark but the great unknown is darker, and before it one shrinks cowering and dismayed.

This paradoxical longing and fear is far more common than is ordinarily supposed. A minister friend who was for months in the grip of this experience (without its being suspected by his parishioners) has told me that during this time he never conducted a funeral without the most conflicting personal emotions. On the one hand, he envied the person in the coffin and felt that he would have given anything he had, could he have honorably exchanged places with the deceased. With another part of him he shrank with horror from the day of his own death, when another would have to be saying similar words over his body. Yet all the while he was normal enough to project himself sympathetically into the grief of the bereaved and to go through the service, not altogether perfunctorily, but with a sense of his high calling as a minister of the gospel. Something like Bunyan's "battle of the texts" must have gone on within him; for sometimes such a funeral service left him completely devastated, shattered with nervous exhaustion, while again it pulled him temporarily out of himself and into a sense of the sustaining sublimity of Christian faith.

What we have here is an abnormal accentuation of certain perennial human tendencies. We must, therefore, look more deeply into the eternal problem and challenge of death.

II

The one wholly inescapable fact for every human being is that he must die. It is normal to marry, to beget children, to have friends, to work, to acquire material possessions—but it is not inevitable. It is the common lot of man to experience pain—we are told that man is made for trouble "as the sparks fly upward"—but there are some persons who from birth to death seem largely if not wholly to escape it. It is man's privilege to find enjoyment in life, but there are some who, through outward circumstance or inner conflict, seem never to be happy. The only thing we must all do is, sooner or later, to die.

In this fact man shares the lot of every living creature. But with a difference. Animals, like human beings, have a biological urge to live; they fight tenaciously for life for themselves and, in the higher forms, for their young. But, so far as can be observed, animals below man have no prevision of the future which would lead them either to long for death or to create a philosophy of resistance to it. Animals do not commit suicide nor do they yearn for immortality.

It is man's glory—which, inverted, becomes his curse —that death for him is far more than a biological event. Try as he may to make of it purely a physical fact, his higher spiritual impulses refuse to accept it as such. It means the cutting off or the continuance of all that is most precious to him, and he must have an answer.

Hence the necessity of some philosophy of death, and the appearance of belief in immortality in all the religions of mankind.

The inevitability of death places before man both great certainty and great uncertainty. While there is nothing surer than death, there is little that is more unpredictable than the time and manner of its coming. As Benjamin Franklin commented, "Nothing is certain but death and taxes." This might equally well be, "Nothing is more *uncertain*." Though man's uneasiness from the latter source is not to be lightly esteemed in time of global war and unlimited spending, our uncertainty regarding the tenure of life itself far exceeds all other hazards that life presents.

Ordinarily, in a relatively stable social situation, this fact does not trouble us greatly. "We must all die sometime; yes, but what of it? Why worry till your time comes?" Such disinterestedness is the usual attitude, particularly with young people, and probably it is a wholesome attitude. Nothing is to be gained by abnormal preoccupation with death. But when an accident occurs and the sudden death of someone who is known and loved shocks the individual into consciousness of his own mortality, he begins to think, and often to flounder.

Multiply this a millionfold, and one gets the present situation. When war disturbs the normal life expectancy of millions and abruptly forces both them and their loved ones to confront the possibility of dying, the result is inner chaos of far-reaching proportions. This means not merely fear of death but a great wonder and confusion about it. Though there is no way of meas-

uring inner against outer upheavals, the social abnormalities of the present are probably not of greater seriousness than the lack of inner moorings. The Christian
gospel must say something about death which has the
ring of assurance, or it cannot get the ear of the multitudes whose primary, unvoiced question is, "If a man
die, shall he live again?"

III

In view of how deeply imbedded the belief in personal
immortality is in Christian thought, one may be surprised to discover how few passages in the New Testament deal directly with it. There is Jesus' great promise that "in my Father's house are many mansions."
There is the magnificent ode to immortality in the fif-
teenth chapter of First Corinthians—the only real attempt in the Bible to deal theologically with the relation
of the "body celestial" to the "body terrestrial." In the
last two chapters of Revelation is the sublime vision of
the new heaven and the new earth, where "death shall
be no more; neither shall there be mourning, nor crying,
nor pain, any more"; where before the throne of God
and of the Lamb "his servants shall serve him; and they
shall see his face"; where "there shall be night no more;
. . . for the Lord God shall give them light: and they
shall reign for ever and ever." There are overtones of
the expectancy of immortality throughout the New
Testament—as in John 3:16, where we find God's promise of everlasting life to those who believe. But, from the
standpoint of proportionate space, the demands and
assurances given for this life far exceed those for the

next. Most burial manuals contain all of these passages within the compass of a few pages.

Why has personal immortality occupied so central a place in Christian faith? There are a number of reasons. For one thing, Christianity was born in the resurrection experience of the early disciples. Disheartened and discouraged at the loss of their leader, they were about to go back to their fishing nets, saying sadly, "We hoped that it was he who should redeem Israel." Then something happened! It convinced them indubitably that their leader was not dead but was in their midst as their living Saviour. "Now hath Christ been raised from the dead." "Because I live, ye shall live also." "O death, where is thy victory? O death, where is thy sting? . . . Thanks be to God, who giveth us the victory through our Lord Jesus Christ." Such words became the rallying cry of the fellowship that formed the Christian Church. Thence came faith and hope. They are still words of high assurance to the great company of Christ's followers. What they say eternally to the Christian is, "Though men may do their worst, God reigns victorious over sin and death."

But this is not our only witness. Even without the record of Christ's resurrection, Christianity would in all probability have made personal immortality a central tenet of its faith. It belongs with the kind of God and the understanding of man which Jesus not only taught but demonstrated.

It is the Christian faith that God is our Father. It is irrational to suppose that a God of fatherly love and sustaining power, who has made man in his own image and who loves all men as his children, could let men's lives be abruptly cut off without hope. A God who would let the millions of helpless victims of this present war be snuffed out utterly would not be the God of Jesus, nor of our own best human insights. Without the persepective of immortality there is no real answer to the problem of unmerited pain.

There are many who say they do not care greatly for immortality for themselves and who doubt their own worthiness to survive. This judgment may be prompted by either pessimism or humility. But, leaving this question aside, for no one can be fully objective about himself, can one say this about another whom he loves? The fact is, he cannot. Nor about humanity in general, if one puts upon human personality the estimate of Christian faith. Man is not "like the beasts that perish," and, however much men may treat other men as beasts, we know through Christ that God cannot. Because man is God's supreme creation, a creature of infinite worth and dignity, it is irrational to suppose God shatters ruthlessly his handiwork. And because with all our faults and frailties we are still God's children, we can know our destinies are safe within his enduring care.

Of the many things outside the Bible that have been written on immortality, three stand out in my memory as stating the case more aptly than I have found it elsewhere. One is Tennyson's great lines in *In Memoriam*:

> Thou wilt not leave us in the dust:
> Thou madest man, he knows not why;
> He thinks he was not made to die;
> And thou hast made him: thou art just.

Another, though now old, is less familiar. When Professor George Herbert Palmer of Harvard was prompted to comment on the early death of his talented wife Alice Freeman Palmer, he wrote: "Though no regrets are proper for the manner of her death, who can contemplate the fact of it and not call the world irrational, if out of deference to a few particles of disordered matter it excludes so fair a spirit?" [1] Though one man may speak as a poet and another as a philosopher, any may find his grief assuaged by confidence in God's steadfast wisdom, justice, and love.

The third, from our own time, is a choice passage in Paul Geren's *Burma Diary*. Ministering in great danger to the bomb-stricken people of Burma, he finds himself saying to them, "God keep you." Others say this to him, and he answers to those he loves, "God *will* keep me." We had better let him explain:

What I mean by this is that God will keep us from the ultimate evil. That ultimate evil is not death. If I were hit by a bomb or a shell, I as I died and they who love me must not think of it as God's failure to keep me. To be kept by God means to be in His love whether living or dying, being hit or escaping. . . . The ultimate evil would be the absence of love. A life outside it would be more evil than a death in it. While we may not be delivered from evils, if God keeps us we shall be delivered from Evil.[2]

Immortality does not mean mere endless duration. Were it a bare extension of existence, it might be end-

[1] Quoted by Harry Emerson Fosdick in *The Assurance of Immortality*, Macmillan, 1913, p. 8.
[2] Harper, 1943, p. 30.

less tedium. It means, rather, a quality of life dominated by love and lived in God's presence. It is significant that the majestic word "I am the resurrection, and the life" stands in the Gospel of John, where the primary emphasis is on a way of life which begins here and is deathless. To be saved by faith in Christ means to enter into an imperishable fellowship with God in Christ.

Regarding the precise nature of the immortal life we must not be too bold. God has not revealed to us the whole mystery. We now see many things "through a glass darkly," and must wait for more light until we see him "face to face." It is consistent with what we know of God through Christ to believe that in the life beyond there will be continuance of the individual soul, fellowship with those we love, a lifting of earthly chains of pain and suffering, a chance to grow in the things of Christ, the glory of God's nearer presence. Though we should like to know much more and be able to "understand all mysteries," if we can have the assurance of God's care for our loved ones and ourselves, it is all we need.

To have these gifts would be heaven; to be cut off from them, our worst punishment. "Whatsoever a man soweth, that shall he also reap"—since this word holds true so clearly in this life, it may well be true of the next. To reject Christ and his way is to plunge ourselves, as we are now witnessing, into fires of conflict that lead to misery, darkness, and destruction. To follow Christ is to find that abundant life which means entrance into the victory of God's eternal Kingdom. Whether for time or eternity, the way of Christ is the way of salvation.

IV

For several pages now we have been talking about the Christian hope of immortality without reference to our distinctive problem. It is time to say what bearing all this has on the experience of the dark night.

The most important conclusion to be drawn is that there is no reason either to fear or to covet death.

If our destinies, whether for this life or the next, are in the keeping of an all-wise, all-loving God, then death, when it comes, means the entrance into a larger life. It means, as the familiar symbolism has it, passage through an open door into a larger room wherein God's presence gleams more radiantly. It means being lifted out of our earth-bound lives and into more glorious opportunities to grow toward "the measure of the stature of the fulness of Christ." The attainment of immortality is something to be greeted neither with dirges of mourning nor with any light disregard of the human grief of separation but with full-throated anthems of rejoicing at God's gift of eternal fellowship. Perhaps this is something of what Paul meant when he said, "To me to live is Christ, and to die is gain."

But is this experience to be hastened by taking matters into human hands? Most decidedly not. As the author of Ecclesiastes has it, "For everything there is a season, and a time for every purpose under heaven: a time to be born, and a time to die. . . . He hath made everything beautiful in its time: also he hath set eternity in their heart." To hasten birth before its time is to destroy life; to hasten death is to destroy life's richness. Much reticence is in order with regard to ascribing to God's will every premature or violent death. But the opposite is certain. It is *never* God's will that an individual take his own life prematurely or violently. To do so is neither "beautiful in its time" nor in keeping with the overtones of eternity that God has set in the human heart.

Nor is the attempt to escape efficacious! However much mystery shrouds "the great beyond," it seems clear that, though death may bring release from the chains of the body, there can be no flight from the soul. What is within the soul—not as a temporary accompaniment of the self but as its permanent and distinctive character—we must carry with us. There is a note of urgency more poignant than fear of the traditional hell in the thought that whatever we do, we must go on living with ourselves forever.

Suicide is not something to be horrified about, as if it were a shocking disgrace or a heinous form of sin. Those who take this step are seldom, if ever, in normal control of their faculties, and ought to be understood rather than condemned. But it is something to be gravely concerned about. It is life's major tragedy, for it means the inversion and denial of the God-given privilege to live.

What, then, should one say to himself if he feels tempted to curtail his life? (What one says to himself is apt to be more potent than what others say.) Among many uncertainties, some facts are certain: Self-destruction is *cowardly*. It is *selfish*. It is *presumptuous*.

It is *unlovely*. It is *self-defeating*. It is *unchristian*. It is the will of God that every sufferer bear as bravely as he can what he has to endure in this life, and await the future, whether earthly or heavenly, with steadfast hope.

It is our glory and our fate that what we do, and prize, and live for in this life stands in direct continuity with the next. The central meaning of eternal life, as the author of the Fourth Gospel so clearly saw, is that in the vista of eternity one can hear Christ say in any circumstance, "Let not your heart be troubled: believe in God, believe also in me." Death is life's fulfillment, the harvesting in God's time of what we sow and water in the present. As we cannot by flight evade the darkness of the soul, so neither darkness nor the shadow of death can hide us from God's sight. The times are in his hand, and in his keeping our treasure is secure.

Chapter VI

Body and Spirit

WE ARE READY NOW TO TRY TO POINT THE WAY OUT OF
darkness. That there *is* a way out is the conviction which
gives this book its only justification. Not all find it. But
many have, and others can.

Nobody knows how many in Christian history have
been engulfed by this experience and have had their
lives permanently warped. Belief that one has committed "the unpardonable sin" has meant, for some, lasting
melancholia. Many others have lived on under strain—
nervous, fretful, depressed—to be a continuing problem to themselves and to those about them. But the
great mystics and saints who have passed through to
come out on the farther side are unanimous in their testimony that the dark night is a purifying experience—
a part of the divine process of refinement by fire that
the dross may be burned away. So it has proved with
many ordinary folk. Though none would choose the
night, many have rejoiced in it after the dawn. Evelyn
Underhill says of it: "This 'great negation' is the sort-
ing-house of the spiritual life. . . . Those who go on are

the great and strong spirits, who do not seek to *know,* but are driven *to be.*" [1]

The way to release and to spiritual power is, obviously, to get at the roots of the experience, eradicate them, and put something constructive in their place. As the book of Ecclesiastes puts it, there is "a time to plant, and a time to pluck up that which is planted." For "radical" treatment, some things must be pulled up by the roots.

But what roots? As has been previously indicated, the phenomenon we are considering is both sin and illness. In either case we must overcome evil with good. But does this mean evil *impulses* or evil *conditions?*

In most instances, it means both. Therefore, the individual must work from both ends at once. If he is inclined to be a hypochondriac, pitying himself and blaming others, he had better do some serious soul searching and get a conscience. But if he already has too much conscience—or, to be more accurate, a distorted conscience—he had better stop his self-accusation, get the best advice he can as to what ails him, then act upon it with his head up. The sinners ought not to try to find alibis, and the sick ought not to be tortured with remorse.

Since all kinds of persons may read this book, the author is puzzled to know from which end to begin! There are several types of causation—physiological, emotional, environmental, moral. They are intimately interwoven. We shall take them up in sequence. It is to be hoped that if anyone reads this chapter and feels

[1] *Mysticism*, p. 454. Her chapter on the dark night is the fullest and most discerning treatment in any contemporary literature.

exonerated, he will also read the next two and be convicted of sin.

I

If a person is upset by nervous tension, what are his physical symptoms? He is apt to be tired, listless, unable to muster the energy for what he formerly did with ease. He has trouble getting to sleep, tossing much of the night and becoming the more uneasy at the thought of all he has to do next day. Or he wants to sleep all the time, and has to fight the temptation to flop on the davenport or bed if he comes within sight of it. In either case he wakes up in the morning more tired than when he went to bed. Or perhaps he has energy enough to last a couple of hours, but drags around the rest of the day. Work is a burden, and life is a drab existence.

Our patient begins to have mysterious pains, more often than elsewhere in his abdomen. His stomach muscles tighten up; he gets indigestion; his elimination becomes irregular. He wonders if a good laxative will not fix him up. He tries it, but feels no better. He wonders if maybe he is getting a gastric ulcer or colitis. (Perhaps he is, but probably not yet.) Or maybe a cancer. He tries to forget this possibility; but the more he tries, the more he thinks about it.

Or the pains strike to his heart. Without warning, a stabbing pain in his "ticker" stops him short in his tracks. It passes after a little, but leaves him wondering. A pain in one's heart is nothing to fool with! Lots of people die of a heart attack. One had better take out some more life insurance if the company's doctor will pass him.

Or he is short of breath. He tried to run half a block for a bus yesterday. He made it, but his head swam and he panted all the way downtown. Lungs, maybe? Or more heart symptoms? There must be something wrong. . . .

Or the pain settles in his head. His eyes hurt, and he has a dull headache all the time. Perhaps his glasses need changing. He visits the oculist, has a fiendish time getting used to his new glasses, and keeps on having a headache. He begins to wonder if maybe he has a brain tumor.

Or the pain lodges in his back. When he writes or drives a car for any length of time he gets a "pain in the neck" that gives savage realism to what was formerly a mild metaphorical expression. Sometimes there is a knife stabbing him in the hollow of his back. He can sit down all right, but then it hurts to get up. He can stand fairly comfortably in a half stoop, but when he tries to straighten up he gets what his grandfather used to call "a crick in the back." He must be getting old. Or maybe there is something wrong with his kidneys, as the patent-medicine ads suggest. People do die of Bright's disease.

Or the pains aren't anywhere in particular, but just all over him. Yes, his feet more than anywhere else. He has a closet full of shoes, but they all hurt him. Why aren't shoes made, he wonders, that fit the human foot? He visits a chiropodist, then an orthopedist, who tell him to go home and forget his feet.

Meanwhile his disposition is bad, worse than he ever knew it to be. He sputters if the coffee is not quite right, or if dinner is not ready on the dot when he gets home. The noise of the kids "drives him nuts," and he wonders why Mary, with nothing much else to do, can't keep them still. He says so frankly, and she gets hurt at his lack of appreciation. Then he gets remorseful, and wonders why a little pain should make him such a crab.

By this time he is sure there is something radically wrong with him. Nobody has all this exhaustion and pain for nothing! The thing to do is to take a week off, go to the hospital, and have a thorough combing over. He does so, with varying results.

Up to this point the story is much the same whether our patient does, or does not, have some organic disturbance. The chances are at least even that, after his week at the hospital, the doctors will dismiss him with the cheerful assurance that there is nothing wrong with him. If he will take a little more rest and recreation and not worry so much, he will be all right. Angry and chagrined, he goes home grumbling at the doctors' stupidity, at his own for having trusted them and spent his money for nothing, and at the world's coldness for refusing to believe that he is sick. He *knows* he does not imagine these pains!

II

If the doctors are right, the rest of the story belongs later. But if some minor organic disturbance is upsetting his nerves, what is most likely to be the matter?

Quite a variety of things, short of the dire premonitions of our patient, could account for the way he feels. Faulty posture is a common cause of strain on the back, feet, and abdominal organs, and consequently on the whole system. The strains from sway-back and protruding abdomen, particularly in connection with the corpulence of middle life, can so throw one's spiritual as well as physical stature out of balance as to make the grace of God seem inaccessible. If one toes out conspicuously when he walks, there is a distortion of the pelvic structure that lets the organs within it sag. One may get away with it—or one may not.

A metabolism of far below or above normal indicates thyroid trouble, with exhaustion from too little secretion into the system from this important gland, and hyperactivity and restlessness from too much. Nobody knows how many millions of people in the world's history have been accused of laziness when a little thyroid accurately administered would have fixed them up. If one's blood count is below the low normal, the chances are that anemia is sapping his vitality, and he needs iron in his diet and more fresh air. Perhaps his diet in general is wrong, particularly if he is overeating or getting too much starch. He needs then to muster enough self-discipline to eat more regularly and more abstemiously, use plenty of fresh vegetables, and—as the radio lets nobody forget—take vitamins. Nutrition is basic to spiritual as to physical health.

The trouble may lie in one of our patient's earliest guesses—the simple but devastating malady of constipation. Or the alimentary canal may be all right and there may still be toxins in the system that more restful sleep or more zestful exercise would help to throw off.

A blood test may reveal the presence of a bacterial infection. If this is causing incipient arthritis or a generally toxic condition, the thing to do is obviously to locate its source and clean it out. The abiding place of the little demons that make one feel "like the devil" is often far from obvious! But it must be sought.

The glands that regulate the supply of sex harmones to the body have a great deal to do with one's disposition. Pregnancy can build up or devastate a woman's morale. Puberty is often a hard time for both adolescents and their parents because it causes drastic emotional as well as physical changes. If our patient is either a man or a woman in the neighborhood of fifty, all sorts of bad feelings, both physical and emotional, can be related to the changes of this period. The menopause, in its more subtle emotional aspects, is little understood by most of those who pass through it or by their families; the male climacteric, even less. Many a domestic tension, leading to domestic tragedy, could be avoided if it were better understood.

Once established, a vicious circle intensifies these troubles. Nervous tension causes pain, and pain causes nervous tension, thus slowing down the naturally curative processes of the body. Low thyroid causes fatigue, and fatigue in turn lowers metabolism. The more one needs exercise, the less inclined one is to want to take it. If one's posture is poor he thinks, though falsely, that he cannot change it. If one has been eating improperly, the chances are that "he likes his stomach" and resents discipline. So with most of the other factors mentioned.

About the only thing one does willingly is to take pills, for these cost only money and not self-control.

If one has a competent doctor, great miracles can be wrought by the right medicine and regimen. But the doctor cannot do everything. What is needed most is right living, which means right working, playing, eating, sleeping, resting, as well as right thinking and a good conscience.

III

Suppose, now, we assume that the doctors at the hospital were right when they said that the patient has nothing organic the matter with him. He is "sound as a dollar." What, then, *is* the matter with him?

In the first place, let it be clear that his pains are not imaginary. They hurt as much as if the X ray had revealed a broken bone or diseased tissue. Nobody ought sneeringly to insinuate that he is making them up to attract pity or evade effort. The patient has a right to be provoked if his family or friends, more pleased than he is at the medical report, say patronizingly, "I told you so. I've thought all along it was just in your mind."

Also, it needs to be clear that both the cause and cure, though related to emotional conflict, are nevertheless in part physiological. Nervous tension has recorded its presence in hundreds of fine muscles all over the body. By continually tensing these muscles, even in sleep, and thus causing them to work overtime, it has accelerated catabolism and slowed down the energy-building forces of the body. There will be no return to vibrant health until the patient relaxes enough to let nature do some building.

Such relaxation depends much on one's state of emotional satisfaction, and of this more presently. But it depends also on certain bodily habits which can be acquired by anybody who knows how and takes the trouble to practice. There are excellent books which tell how physiological relaxation is done, though no book will supply the will power to keep practicing.[2] Even without a book, one does the biggest part of it when he so orders his life as to find time to lie flat on his back a half hour at least once a day, and lets himself "go negative." He must lie still, without the twitches he ordinarily indulges in to try to get comfortable, for nervousness is largely a frustrated attempt to find comfort. But he must not hold himself rigid. He must, as far as he is able, *do nothing.* If he can find his tensions— the books show where to look for them—he must consciously relax them. So interrelated is the body that if you will raise one wrist with the hand drooping, find the resulting tension in the upper arm, then drop the whole arm loosely on the couch, tensions will be released not only in this arm but all over the body.[3] If one cannot locate one's tensions but simply lies quietly in a horizontal position, nature will take care of a great many of them.

The rub comes in the fact that the people who need most to take such periods of relaxation are the ones so busy they think they cannot spare the time. Actually,

[2] Among the best are Edmund Jacobson, *You Must Relax,* Whittlesey House, 1934, and *You Can Sleep Well,* Whittlesey House, 1938; David Fink, *Release From Nervous Tension,* Simon & Schuster, 1943; Josephine Rathbone, *Relaxation,* Teachers College, 1943.

[3] For diagrams see Edmund Jacobson, *You Must Relax,* Whittlesey House, 1942.

much more time is gained through increased efficiency than is lost by periodic resting. But nobody will believe this for himself (however freely he admits it for others) until illness and the doctor's say-so force it on his attention. Then he knows privately (though he still hates terribly to admit it!) that if he had decided this for himself it would have been cheaper in time and money.

Such muscular relaxation obviously gives the entire body a better chance to function normally and thus to build up resistance to illness and fatigue. Another aspect of the matter is less obvious but very important.

There is a close relation between the muscles and glands and the autonomic nervous system of the body. This autonomic (sometimes called sympathetic) nervous system has connections running to all parts of the body. It is very susceptible to impulses from the subconscious mind, and is connected with the central nervous system but not fully under its control. This is why emotional states with such accompanying bodily changes as blushing, weeping, high-pitched tones, shaking knees, and general exhaustion are only partially subject to control by the will. Multiply such changes and prolong the effects, and serious physical results ensue from emotional tensions. Reverse the process, release the muscular tensions, and the emotional states become subdued.

How this works is all very intricate, and not very well understood. It has been popularized in the following imaginary conversation between a psychiatrist and a man whose illness was directly caused by emotional conflict:

"The interbrain cannot be reached directly," the psychiatrist went on. "It has its own private telephone exchange, so that messages from conscious thought cannot reach it. That is why talking and arguing can't cure nervousness. But it does receive messages from your muscles and other parts of the body. The interbrain does understand the language of the body. Therefore, reeducation of your misbehaving interbrain must be indirect.

"When your muscles are tense, they send messages of disturbances to the interbrain. And your interbrain responds to these messages. Tense muscles will stir up a storm within the interbrain that can tie your stomach in a knot and make your heart race.

"You can learn to control your muscles. You can teach them to relax. Your relaxed muscles will train your interbrain in new habits, normal habits, and your body will work again in the way that it was meant to work. A man with relaxed muscles can't have habitual interbrain trouble, and he just can't be nervous." [4]

IV

We leave now the physiology of the situation and move more directly into the question of emotional conflicts. What sort of situations induce persistent nervous tension and thus, in a spiritual sense, the dark night?

Much has been written of the more overt forms of emotional conflict and their disturbing effects. Here belongs the story of the man who wants to make money by any means he can and still be thought an honest man, of the woman who wants to be petted and is made ill by her subconscious so that her husband will dance attend-

---

[4] "Your Emotional Conflict," by David H. Fink, M.D., in *Good Housekeeping*, April, 1944.

ance. It has become a commonplace of the newer psychology that childhood experiences often have a lasting effect on personality by causing inhibitions and complexes that are primarily forms of emotional conflict. These may run into physical illness; they are bound to cause unhappiness. In exaggerated forms they produce delinquency—juvenile or otherwise—and serious nervous disturbances.

Of such conflicts I do not propose to say much. Only a competent psychiatrist or consulting psychologist is fitted to deal with them in their extreme forms. For milder cases much general information is already available, for any number of authoritative books deal with them.[5] What we are more concerned with is the development of disrupting conflicts in religiously sensitive persons who desire, as far as they are able, to discover and do the will of God.

It may be helpful to return for a moment to the saints and mystics of the past. Knowing nothing of present-day psychological diction, they were in many cases remarkably keen analysts of the ways of human nature.

When one looks into the inner experience of those who have left their record of the dark night,[6] several factors stand out as causes. Among them are exhaustion, anxiety, excessive introspection, and a frustrated search for spiritual enjoyment.

It is highly probable that there were physical causes

[5] Among the best are Karen Horney, *The Neurotic Personality of Our Time;* Anton Boisen, *The Exploration of the Inner World;* and Fritz Künkel, *Let's Be Normal.* See Appendix A for other titles.

[6] See Chapters II and III.

in some instances. What the saints saw in their overt illnesses were punishments and trials sent by the Lord. Doubtless many times they were sick without knowing it. The evidence is meager here. But one form of illness, current in Christian leaders to the present, most of them had.

When one has worked excessively at his religious life, whether in works of meditation and prayer or in deeds of service, there comes inevitably a swingback. It is an obvious fact, but one which most ardent souls must learn from experience, that one cannot indefinitely expend either physical or psychic energy. When in the grip of a great enthusiasm one attempts to do so, nature reminds us that the soul is tethered to a body. Most of the mystics, for all of their hours at prayer, seem to have been very intense persons. Even the rapture of the vision of God takes its toll, and one finds in the story of such a joyous, single-minded soul as St. Francis great periods of weeping which injured his eyesight. Sometimes because their praying was not sufficiently balanced with labor, sometimes because their labors were too much for frail bodies in a day that knew little of medical care or physical comforts, they wore themselves out. Depression was a natural consequence.

As one reads their records it is clear that those who passed through the dark night were very much concerned about themselves. They worried too much about their souls for their own good. But this does not get to the bottom of the situation, which is that they worried *because they thought they had lost the one thing most needful*. To one who has dedicated his soul to God and has felt the life-giving sense of God's presence, there is no deeper hell than to feel bereft of it. To take this nonchalantly, if it were possible, would be sin; when one is the kind of person we are considering, it is not possible. The dark night is fundamentally an anxiety neurosis, which, according to Dr. Karen Horney, is the root of "the neurotic personality of our time."

This brings us to the crucial factor. Those who passed through it record with one voice their belief, in retrospect, that God had led them to it because in his love he desired to call them to a higher level of the life of devotion. What they had to undergo was an experience of "self-naughting" in which they must learn to give up for God not only worldly but even spiritual pleasures. In the words of the *Theologia Germanica*, they must "be simply and wholly bereft of self." They must learn to "lie still under God's hand," to surrender "the I, the me, the mine," to live for God alone.

One does not catch what the mystics meant if he supposes that this self-surrender refers to ordinary carnal selfishness, such as one must repent of before one becomes a Christian and keep repenting of. It is something far more subtle and devastating. It means pride in being well thought of as a servant of God, satisfaction in being able to do well the works of God. But at a still deeper level of self-centeredness it means enjoyment of God's presence in prayer—the quest for spiritual blessings through communion with him, not for the love of God but for one's own satisfaction. What the mystics saw, after God had used the painful experience of the dark night to open their eyes, was that to enjoy God

111

before one glorifies him is to lose the assurance of his presence.

V

What does all this mean, in the more familiar circumstances of contemporary life? It means that in religious matters, as in secular, one wants to, but cannot, "have his cake and eat it." The only release is to give up attempting the impossible.

To illustrate: Most religious persons, especially ministers, teachers, and those in professions that deal directly with persons, want to serve God and the people. Being sensitive to human need, they want to give all the service they can. If they were insensitive and callous, they could be unmoved by the sight of human sin and suffering, and could live on comfortably immune from nervous strain. But this is just what they are not. They want so much to serve that they end up by curtailing the strength by which to serve.

The next stage in the disruption of morale in the highly moral is the conflict between what one *was* and *is,* between what one *could* do and what one now *can* do. Very few people who have previously lived a highly active and efficient life can take gracefully the necessity of slowing down. They either fume against fate or fume at themselves for being such a dud, such a nitwit, such a—here it is helpful if one has versatility in vocabulary! Being what they are, and not persons of bovine complacency, they worry at having lost their capacity to get things done. They worry at becoming a burden and a problem to others, whereas previously they had been able not only to take care of themselves but to do a little lifting. Still more, they worry at not being able to find in God the peace they had formerly thought always available for the asking.

This leads on to the self-interrogation which is rarely free from self-accusation. The "cake" one wants to have and also eat is a clear conscience and at the same time the discovery of fault, which by necessity gives a verdict of "not clear." Self-pity gets so mixed up with self-condemnation that nervous tension and moral confusion are inevitable. It is like trying to hold open a door and slam it shut at the same time.

To add to the conflict, one wants at the same time to be both happy and unhappy. Of course, consciously one wants only to be happy. Subconsciously, the only channels that have free course in one's badly damned up nervous system are those carrying depressed emotions, and the psyche, like any stream, follows the path of least resistance. If the sufferer felt better, he might exert some will power and redirect the course of his unhappy, anxious thought. But that is just the trouble: he does not have the will power. The gratuitous advice of his well-meaning friends only increases the inner turmoil, for he knows as well as they that he ought to "buck up and stop worrying." As Dr. Fosdick puts it pointedly:

There are types of melancholia where it is positively dangerous to urge the victim by trying hard to overcome his despondency. In neurasthenia, where shock, overstrain, or chronic fatigue has brought on genuine nervous prostration, trying hard is the worst possible therapy. It is precisely what one tries hard with that is sick.[7]

In this plight some things—one may truly thank God —are still effective and curative. One is the physiological relaxation suggested earlier in this chapter, and the use of whatever medical helps the body requires. Another is limited work—not idleness, to give Satan a chance for filling empty hands—but enough congenial work to direct one's attenion outward. A resource of incalculable value is the support of understanding human companionship. A wife or a friend, simply by loving and never letting down, has saved many a man in this state from suicide or insanity. If one cannot do anything else to help the sufferer, one can learn when to speak and when to be silent. One can go on patiently believing in him, forgiving sharp words, overlooking slights, anticipating needs, and speaking words of appreciation whenever these can be spoken without hypocrisy.

But this is not all. "Underneath are the everlasting arms." It is as the troubled soul enters into a deeper, more revealing, more encompassing sense of God's presence that dawn follows the night. It is when one ceases to demand of God health, or happiness, or usefulness, or any of his gifts, but asks only for God himself, that the light breaks and the shadows flee away.

[7] *On Being a Real Person,* Harper, 1943, p. 188.

Chapter VII

The Sins of Society

IN THE PREVIOUS CHAPTER WE TOOK A GLANCE AT THE physical causes of psychic depression, and at such spiritual factors as derive basically from the individual's self-expenditure for what he believes to be the will and work of God. It is necessary now to look at some environmental factors and inner distortions which exist only because of somebody's sin.

To say "somebody's sin" is ambiguous; for, as in the case of global war, the "somebodies" responsible, as well as those victimized, may mount into the many millions. There is, we have previously contended, no sharp line to be drawn between misfortune and moral guilt in the phenomenon we are discussing. To burn out one's body even for the highest ends is to sin against the "temple of the Holy Spirit." Yet there is a recognizable difference between this and crude selfishness. So is there a difference between physical illness that upsets spiritual balance and evil elements in the social situation.

Everything we shall mention in this chapter is accentuated by the strains of war. However, we shall speak first of long-range matters persistently present in so-called times of peace.

In the issues to be discussed much needs to be done by society to remedy conditions. But in almost every instance the individual caught in a bad situation can himself do something to better it. In order to avoid the supineness of self-pity, it is important to recognize this fact. To be a victim of circumstances does not mean to be a helpless victim. Whatever one can do, one ought to do. What one cannot change, one ought to accept with as much patience and fortitude as he can, looking to God for grace to endure it without bitterness. It is the function of religion to enable men in evil situations to do what they can and endure what they must.

I

The most fertile source of psychic disturbances is in the family. It is one of the deep paradoxes of our existence that the family, center and source of the best in human love, chosen by our Lord to symbolize God's loving relationship to his children, is likewise the lurking place of the most diabolical conflict and misery.

It begins—where? As modern psychiatry keeps reminding us, most adult difficulties can be traced to unfortunate childhood experiences. These are often the product of parental unhappiness, and such frustration in the home usually goes back to something wrong in the marriage that established the home. But whatever was wrong in the marriage is in turn the product of something back of that. So it turns out to be biological and psychological truth that the sins of the fathers are visited upon the children to the third and fourth generation. It is a mistake to ignore such causal sequences; it is equally a mistake to suppose that everything can be explained by them.

Many of the characteristics of the dark night are attributable, at least in part, to infantilisms, that is, to the failure to achieve psychic and spiritual maturity as one grows up biologically. We noted the tendency to self-pity and craving for sympathy; to self-condemnation and an exaggerated sensitiveness; to loneliness, but also the tendency to repulse overtures of friendship. It is not difficult to see here an adult version of certain common childhood experiences. One wants still the cuddling and kissing of hurt places that he had when he fell and hurt himself and ran to Mother to have her make it well. Or, as a child one told a lie, or stole something, or otherwise offended against what society demanded; he was scolded angrily—perhaps put to bed supperless or beaten. He knew he had done wrong, but with remorse was mingled a rankling sense of rebellion at the pain of punishment. The culprit-victim recoiled by withdrawing into a dark corner of his heart to suffer in the loneliness of misunderstanding.

Opinions differ as to the importance to be attached to single, long-buried incidents. Some psychiatrists regard them as crucial clues to adult disturbances. This emphasis can be overdone. No child is brought up ideally, and a welter of experience could be uncovered in anybody's past to account for almost anything in the present. Nature, if given a chance, has wonderfully restorative powers to heal wounds of the spirit as well as the body. Awareness of this fact should save conscientious parents from much distraction of fussiness over their own potential errors.

Yet in a general way it is clearly true that "as the twig is bent the tree is inclined." Incidents are chiefly important as an index of habitual trends. An excessive amount of either coddling or condemnation in childhood is bound to leave psychic scars. If one does not have in childhood the understanding friendship, as well as the love, of his parents, he has a head start toward being all his days lonely and inhibited. If one grows up hearing his parents quarrel and has no assurance of security in the home, his outlook on the world is tinctured with insecurity. If one is a sensitive child and this sensitiveness is not channeled into sympathetic concern for others, it will recoil to make him suffer acutely in adult life from imagined slurs and stings. If one does not learn in childhood to give and take, to be co-operative and responsible, one grows up demanding possessions, services, and attention which one is not willing to reciprocate. Most meanness is selfishness, and most selfishness is the natural egocentricity of childhood unripened and uncurbed.

There is a source of much nerve strain in the conflict of the generations that emerges at adolescence. Few parents are wise enough to surrender authority to their growing children in exactly the right way, not too much and not too little, not too soon and not too late. Adolescents must at the same time be shielded like children and given independence like adults. But how? What seems to the younger generation conservatism and inordinate fussiness in their parents raises conflicts at a thousand points, while the apparent unconcern of the young for anything but their own way is heartbreaking to parents who do not understand it. The result is that, although parents and children love each other, they clash, lash out with their tongues, get hurt feelings, seem not to love each other, and all of them "get nerves." There are, of course, deep sources of pride and satisfaction in the achievements of one's children, but these seldom come unmixed with the apprehension which is the counterpart of loving concern.

Such strains are accentuated by the fact that the hardest problems come just at the time when the parents' physical energy is slowing down and outside demands are at their peak. Most of my contemporaries tell me that getting their children through the measles and whooping-cough stage was a trifle compared with getting them through high school and college! When the weddings are over and the last child happily married, one has to recuperate—not from physical activities only, but from the accumulated though often unconscious nerve strain of years of responsibility.

If the young person is unhappily or unwisely married, or if parents try to dominate the new home, or if the families of two generations have to live together, the stage is set for further strains. More conflicts are precipitated, and the lives of all can be permanently warped and hampered. Under these conditions only the most callous or those who are made strong by the grace of God can go forward with skies unclouded. Jokes are cracked about the mother-in-law problem because so many tragedies lie here that we seek unconsciously by levity to cover tragedy.

We have hinted at territory that calls for much further exploration than it has had, namely, the strains peculiar to middle life.[1] It is not accidental that nervous breakdowns come so frequently at this period. One is often surprised to hear of a family that breaks up after twenty or twenty-five years of apparently successful marriage. These circumstances are connected.

The reasons are numerous. There is the factor mentioned a moment ago—depletion of energy with increase in demands, and consequently the undertaking of more work than one can do. There is the pressure of business which takes a man's attention more and more away from his home, and makes his wife feel neglected while he feels inadequately appreciated. There is sexual disturbance in both from glandular changes. There is the fading of her physical beauty, which with certain turbulent inner forces makes him look longingly (even though with the restraints imposed by respectability) at a younger and prettier woman. There is his wife's consequent malaise which is really jealousy, though she hates to recognize it as such; her tears flow at the wrong moments and make him angry. There is his hurt that she cannot trust him, and her hurt that he does not love her as he used to. There is an attempt to patch things up, which only precipitates another scene, with more tears and more sharp words. They decide it may be better hereafter to have separate bedrooms.

[1] See Grace Loucks Elliott, *Women After Forty*, Holt, 1936.

There is her preoccupation—far greater than his—with the strains from the children's baffling behavior, and her self-pity that he expects her to carry the brunt of it. There is his annoyance that she phones him of Bill's being taken to the police station, or of Mary's threat to elope with the butcher's son, just as he is about to close an important deal. He thinks it is her business to attend to such things: she thinks it is his! Both say so frankly, to no advantage. Then later, when the children are on their own, there is a letdown from the necessity of putting up with domestic strains for the children's sake. One begins to wonder if it is worth while to go on in order to keep up appearances.

Meanwhile both he and she, who formerly cut quite a figure socially, are settling down. Everybody takes them pretty much for granted. There is not the exhilaration of an evening out, or even of a vacation in the country, that one formerly had. It seems hardly worth while to get dressed up any more. There is not much to do for recreation but to stay home and rest, and staying at home becomes more and more unrestful. Now that the children are gone, is it really worth while?

If this state of affairs continues for several years, the answer will probably be no. The last chapter of the unpleasant drama has several possible conclusions. There may be a separation, more often a separation by mutual consent than outright divorce. He finds his business keeps him most of the time in another part of the country, or she makes a long visit to the married daughter's to help with the new baby. Or there is a grim determination, come what may, to stick it out. Or as sexual pressures subside there is a truce, and something like an appeasement. Or one or the other gets a nervous breakdown. In rare instances suicide or insanity is precipitated.

The only other alternative is a true reconciliation, based on the recognition of powerful physical and social forces, of fault on both sides, and of the need to do some giving in for the sake of love. This course is the hardest, the most rewarding, and the most needful of the grace of God. It is also the rarest. As lonely, wise Spinoza once said, "All things excellent are as difficult as they are rare."

II

We have not in the preceding section begun to canvass all the inducements to the spiritual disturbances precipitated by strains within the family. But we must leave this field to look at another almost as fertile in the production of tares. This is the vocation in which one spends the greater part of one's waking hours.

In the Oxford Conference Report there is a searching analysis of the points at which a Christian understanding of life is challenged by our present economic system. Among them is the significant item "The Frustration of the Sense of Christian Vocation." A paragraph is worth quoting in full:

A profound conflict has arisen between the demand that the Christian should be doing the will of God in his daily work, and the actual kinds of work which Christians find themselves forced to do within the economic order. With regard to the worker and employee, there is the fact that most of them are *directly* conscious of working for the profit of the employer (and for the sake of their wages) and only *indirectly* conscious of working for any public good; while this fact may in some cases be only part of the mechanism by which the work is done for the public good, the difficulty in some degree remains. Again, there is the fact that at present many workers must produce things which are useless or shoddy or destructive. Finally, one other form of work which seems clearly to be in conflict with the Christian's vocation is salesmanship of a kind which involves deception—the deception which may be no more than insinuation and exaggeration, but which is a serious threat to the integrity of the worker.[2]

There is no aspect of the ministry of the Church in which it has proceeded with greater unrealism than in this matter. As preachers we have assumed, on the whole, even if we did not fully believe it, that the preaching and worship of the Sunday service would somehow carry over into the work of the week. As laymen we have largely proceeded on the assumption that "business is business," and not to be brought too much under the scrutiny of religion. In the medieval church and in the Reformation period considerable emphasis was placed on the need of serving God in and through one's daily vocation.[3] This note we have all but lost. As a consequence, the Church not only stands mainly outside the labor movement, but outside the practical working activities of most of its membership.

[2] Section III, "The Church and the Economic Order," 3 (d).

[3] See my *John Calvin: The Man and His Ethics*, chap. x, for a survey of these movements.

The results are inevitable, and serious. Aside from housewives and farmers, whose hours of labor are not easily calculable, most of the adult members of our churches spend forty to fifty hours a week in some kind of paid employment. If a person spends one hour in worship and spends forty in a secular situation where he is surrounded by influences adverse to everything he hears in church, what happens? The chances are forty to one that the dominant influences in his life are those of his vocation. Only the strongest or the most insensitive can withstand the impact of what they have to do and say and hear all day long five or six days a week.

This is not to imply that vocations are in general corrupting in the grosser sense. Since we have laws against larceny, embezzlement, and other forms of fraud, most people work under conditions reasonably free from overt dishonesty. The trouble lies deeper, in the depersonalized character of our industrial society. It is in the monotony, the speed-up, the cutting of corners, the faster and faster race to beat competitors, that one's physical and psychic energy is sapped. It is the shoddy ideals of associates (to most of whom the Church means nothing), the implicit assumption that money and more business are the end of existence, the dissociation between what one does and any sense of service to God or man, that drains spiritual energies. Add to these factors the awareness—if one lets himself think about it—that one is being party to processes of exploitation of labor, capital, or the public, and nothing but frustration and dull discontent can be expected to ensue.

This is not all. In the past, and to a large extent still,

we have done so little and so poorly in the way of vocational guidance that relatively few people are fully happy in their occupations. Most persons in middle life are now doing what they are doing, not from any well-considered choice, but because twenty or thirty years ago temporary expediency or geographical propinquity, the pull of influential friends or the push of parental pressure, started them along this line. It is now too late to change. Or is it? They wonder, and are continually upset by the strain of indecision. It does not aid their solution that half of them wish "somebody had told me," while the other half blame the bad advice of someone who did tell them. Add to this group those who in their younger years knew what they wanted but could not pursue a coveted profession because of family responsibilities or the lack of opportunity for preparation, and the company of those who are dissatisfied in their work is legion.

The domestic tensions of the previous section impinge on the problem to complicate it further. Since life is all of one piece however much we try to compartmentalize it, persons unhappy at home are usually unhappy at work also. By subconscious rationalizations conflicts within the family are projected into occupational relations, and one finds himself—often without clearly understanding why—getting into tangles, slowing down his efficiency, losing his nerve, his poise, his capacity to "put it over."

What, then, is to be done about these matters? This is clearly a case in which one must do what one can and endure what one must.

The ultimate end toward which all Christians need to work is the remaking of our total economic structure in the direction of making it serve human welfare. God has provided enough for all; we have sadly bungled our use of his gifts. The goods produced, the processes of production, and the consuming power which determines their distribution, need constantly to be brought under the searchlight of the Christian gospel. Change will come only as individuals, both in pulpits and places of business, keep working at it courageously and patiently, and with due regard for differing opinions. Though total change will not come all at once, there is no situation that is completely impervious to change.

Meanwhile Christians are responsible for making the best possible out of every bad situation. There is no single way to do this. But certain questions may well be asked.

If work is irksome, has one prayed about it? Has one really tried to see in this work, with all its distasteful drudgery, a needful service to humanity? If so, it is God's work for the advancement of his Kingdom.

Has one tried to get acquainted with one's associates and find something enriching in them? They too are persons. The most barren soil yields fruit if rightly fertilized.

Has one accepted the fact that this job is the necessary means to the fulfillment of a duty outside of itself? Jesus regarded the care of parents as a service to God taking precedence of a gift laid upon the altar. If the meeting of a human obligation lies clearly in the path of duty, much that is otherwise murky and disagreeable becomes filled with light.

Has one made the best possible use of his leisure? Does one have an avocation as well as a vocation? This does not mean always "improving one's mind," or "getting something done." It may mean this, and it should for the irresponsible. But since the victims of the dark night are apt to be too intense persons anyway, it may mean for them the duty of doing something uncreative, just for the sake of enjoying themselves. For all, it means that a full and rewarding life must have variety, range, and depth of interests. Both creation and recreation are in the normal gamut of existence.

Most of the foregoing has been written with the worker in so-called secular occupations in mind. A further word is in order for the professional religious worker. His problem is not how to find something useful and interesting to do. Rather, it is how to limit his expenditure of strength, how to choose wisely what to do and leave undone, how to keep the irregular and manifold duties of his profession from crowding too heavily on the hours needed for sleep, recreation, and family life. He has to learn how to protect himself from needless interruption, but also how to accept interruption in the midst of his creative labors without getting irritated or upset. He has to have self-confidence but guard against the overconfidence that runs into self-righteousness. He has to expect compliments and appreciation, but learn how to do without them. He has to discipline himself to do a great many unpleasant things cheerfully for the sake of doing the greater work in which his soul rejoices. Failing to learn these things, either his health or his professional usefulness, or both, will pay the penalty.

Whether in secular or religious occupations, we have a long way yet to go before we learn to manage rightly the work side of our existence, and integrate it with our worship. Brother Lawrence has something to teach us at this point. But of this, more later.

III

Some colossal social evils are so directly destructive to nervous stability that one must say about them either very much or very little, and the limits of this book require that it be little. I refer to poverty, race prejudice, and war.

Inadequate economic resources cut into psychic health from many angles. There is, to begin with, the inability of the poor to be "well born" in a physical sense, for the number of births with only midwives in attendance is still appalling. There is a direct correlation between a high infant mortality rate and a low income level. Those children who survive but who get inadequate or improper food or who sleep in ill-ventilated, overcrowded slum tenements have a head start toward nervous disorders. Add to this the play environment that usually goes with poverty and the domestic tensions rarely absent, and all the ingredients of psychic instability are there. What such limitation means, not only in childhood but in the crucial experiences of adolescence, is too familiar a story to require retelling.

Among adults, poverty is not inevitably a curse. If

voluntarily chosen, as by Jesus or St. Francis, it can simplify life by casting off many accretions to make room for essentials. But this is no excuse for complacency before the poverty of others! What it does to most people, even to some who choose underpaid professions like the ministry with their eyes open, is to cause bitterness, rankling discontent, and the curtailment of much that could contribute to the higher life. When it is a matter of one's own inadequate income, the Christian has the double duty of pressing for its increase without becoming grasping or money-minded. When it is a question of another's underpay, there is a clear social obligation to do whatever is possible to lift income to a level commensurate with basic needs.

Just how much anyone needs for health of body and soul is, of course, something for which no exact measure is possible. Every individual ought to have enough for simple but comfortable living, not so much as to encourage idleness and swank. One ought to have enough so that he can, for the most part, forget about money instead of having to be obsessed by concern for it. When this becomes possible for all, earth will be nearer the Kingdom of Heaven than it now is.

IV

Race prejudice is the most persistent demon in our social structure. In poverty and affluence, in peace and war, it lifts its ugly head. Few there are that are wholly free from it, even among the most sensitive and otherwise healthy-minded Christians. Race prejudice is to be found in every church—if not in its official action, in the acts and attitudes of the congregation. It ramifies throughout all social institutions to breed intense personal unhappiness and imperil the peace of the world.[4]

The report of the Delaware Conference states the case regarding America as succinctly as I have found it put. It reads:

In our own country millions of people, especially American Negroes, are subjected to discrimination and unequal treatment in educational opportunities, in employment, wages and conditions of work, in access to professional and business opportunities, in housing, in transportation, in the administration of justice and even in the right to vote.

Back of these words lies an incalculable amount of human misery. I shall not attempt to describe it. I doubt whether anyone who has not been subjected all his life to the limitations and indignities suggested by this list of discriminatory measures can adequately describe how it feels. But with even a little imagination one can grasp what it does to the personality of its victims, particularly its younger victims. The wonder is not that there are outcroppings of bitterness, but that Jews after centuries of persecution and homelessness and Negroes after centuries of slavery and discrimination are as free from bitterness as they are. Nothing but deep roots of religious faith could have saved them from it.

[4] My further convictions on the subject are stated in a chapter entitled "The Racial Issue and the Christian Church" in *The Church and the New World Mind*, the addresses given at the Drake Conference of the Disciples Church, Feb. 1-4, 1944.

V

In the foregoing pages little has been said about war. This omission is deliberate; for, though the experience of the dark night has been greatly accentuated by the war, it was not brought into being by it. It is, however, impossible to leave the subject of its social causes without a further word on this point.

Of the basic evilness of war and its world-wide destructiveness little need here be said. The Oxford Conference said it in words destined to last long when it declared:

War involves compulsory enmity, diabolical outrage against human personality, and a wanton distortion of the truth. War is a particular demonstration of the power of sin in this world and a defiance of the righteousness of God as revealed in Jesus Christ and him crucified.[5]

This being so, what does it do to the spiritual stability of its victims?

There are undoubtedly some persons who under the challenge of a great cause to which to give themselves, and out of the winnowing flames of suffering, have come to deeper undergirding and higher spiritual stature. Brought face to face with loss of this world's possessions, pain, and imminent death, nobody can be indifferent to ultimate issues. That there has been an upturn in religious interest in recent years is an altogether natural consequence of social catastrophe.

But this is one side only. Not only does this fact give no sound basis for optimistic assumptions about the

[5] Section V, "The Universal Church and the World of Nations," 7.

religious interests of returning soldiers; it fails to state how deeply shaken the spiritual life of many persons has been in these times. Suffering, particularly when joined with the break-up of familiar social moorings, embitters and shatters far more people than it refines.

The points at which this occurs can only be suggested. There is the inevitable anxiety one feels for loved ones, from whose safety it is impossible to turn one's thoughts. There is the pain of separation, probably temporary but possibly permanent. The fear of its being permanent clutches ever at one's heart; faith may alleviate but cannot banish it. Fear begets heaviness of spirit, and heaviness more fear.

For those called to give up their careers and enter the armed forces, the resulting physical and mental strain induces turmoil or a stoic acceptance of a dirty job that must be finished. There is a merging of inevitability with uncertainty—the surrender of one's will to colossal forces, but with no clear assurance of what lies ahead. Not only is one's own fate uncertain—one expects that in war—but there is no assurance that it will not all have to be done over in another generation. Besides, though there seems no alternative, there is a large uncertainty that one ought to be doing what one must be doing. It all seems so chaotic—so contrary to what one has been taught all one's life. It is bad to hate and kill, and it is hard to kill without hate. So what? Even strenuous indoctrination fails to banish the question.

Those who resolve this conflict by going to camps for conscientious objectors confront other conflicts. It is not easy to cling resolutely to one's ideals when one's position is misunderstood and one's family stigmatized as well as oneself, when one gets neither pay nor maintenance but must be supported by somebody, when the clothing one brought to camp several years ago gets more and more shabby and less protective, when one spends one's time in boondoggling jobs instead of the "civilian public service" for which one had hoped. Narrow circumstances make for narrowing vision, and one wonders whether it is worth the cost.

There is the serious but relatively painless upheaval of millions shaken from their wonted ways to work in defense industries and other forms of war work, too tired for the most part to think much about God. In war-devastated areas there is the almost unimaginable suffering of millions of refugees and sick, wounded, starving, bombed civilians. There is the indescribable horror of every battle front. In such circumstances it is only natural that, for most men, thoughts of the higher life must yield to doing the job that the moment demands, and surviving if one can.

In the face of such facts only the most superficial optimism could maintain that the cause of religion has been advanced. The war has shown man the need of religion. It has shown that both personal religion and the fellowship of the Church can stand the strains of conflict and give stability under fire. It has not purified the souls of most of its victims, and it has plunged millions into darkness and the shadow of death.

Chapter VIII

The Burden of Our Sin

IN THE TWO PRECEDING CHAPTERS WE HAVE TRACED
some of the more common causes of spiritual depression
arising from physiological and emotional disturbances,
and the precipitation of such emotional conflicts by
factors in the environment that cry out for readjust-
ment. There has been no attempt in our analysis to dis-
sociate these sharply from sin. In fact, we have said
repeatedly that no absolute line can be drawn in such
matters between maladjustment and sin. Nevertheless,
in the areas canvassed thus far, the individual is primarily the victim of forces other than his own will which
disrupt the personality and distort the right function-
ing of body and spirit. There are other situations wherein the sufferer in the dark night is primarily the victim
of his own evil impulses. He has sinned, and "the wages
of sin is death." At these factors we must now look.

Traditional theology has overweighted the Christian
judgment in the direction of calling everything that is
wrong in a person's life by the ugly name of sin. Liberalism, leaning in the opposite direction, has put its major
emphasis on the correction of personal and social maladjustments and the creation of proper conditions for

134

the growth and enrichment of personality. The new orthodoxy has recovered the historic Christian emphasis on sin, but without adequate recognition that, though sin and weakness come mixed in every individual, there is still a real difference between them.

Both the older Christian orthodoxy and the newer type represented by Barth and Niebuhr have been greatly concerned to emphasize man's sinfulness in order to leave no loophole for moral alibis and complacency. In these systems man's weakness or finiteness, though not denied, is made part of his general plight; for, inescapably caught in the toils of sin, man is unable to save himself by his own wisdom or strength. God alone can save us. Liberal theology, keeping closer to the mood of science, has tended to see evil conduct as the product of a chain of causes that ought to be remedied and that *can* be remedied by a right use of our God-given faculties of intelligence and moral sensitiveness.

Each of these views requires to be supplemented by a truth in the other. Sin is real; so is our limitation. We need to be saved from both, and we can be saved only as we respond to what God demands. What we have to do is to understand, sympathize with, and correct weakness and at the same time bear down hard upon sin. However tolerant we need to be toward the sins of others, nobody ought to tolerate his own. As the Prayer Book has it, we are "miserable offenders"; we stand ever in need of God's mercy, and the burden of our sins ought to be intolerable to us.

I

Before examining the special bearing of sin and guilt on our problem, it is again necessary to take a little excursion into theology to be clear as to what we are talking about. What, then, do we mean by sin?

There is no single definition of sin, and no list of sins that could be drawn up would be complete. When we begin looking at the demonic evil forces that assail the human spirit, we see that their name is legion. There are, however, certain marks that give concrete meaning to the term.

In the first place, any act or attitude that is sinful runs counter to the nature of God and the righteous will of God. This is the truth that lies in the often distorted doctrine of human depravity. When we measure even our best acts and aspirations by the standard of God's holy will as revealed in Christ, we all have sinned and come short of the glory of God. The eclipse of the concept of sin during the brief ascendancy of humanistic liberalism was a direct outgrowth of our failure to take seriously God's transcendent holiness and the rigor of his moral demands. When man becomes the measure of all things, we talk of "cultural lags" and "antisocial behavior." When God is restored to his rightful place of primacy in human thought, sin, our ancient enemy, again is seen to be our ever-present and most malignant foe.

In the second place, any sin, whether of overt act or inner attitude, presupposes freedom to do or to be otherwise. To the extent that a person really does what he must do or is what he must be, *and cannot help himself,* to that extent he is victim and not sinner. As nobody is wholly free, so nobody is wholly depraved. But the other side of this comforting truth is that one rarely, if ever, is wholly helpless and therefore free from culpability. In almost every situation there is freedom enough left to do better than one does. Certainly if we view life, not as separate incidents, but as a whole, nobody ever reaches the upper limits of his freedom. In those large areas of choice which God has given us but within which we do not choose according to his will, we sin and stand under his righteous judgment. Thus the correlate of his great gift of freedom is that we are responsible before him for its misuse.

In the third place, sin presupposes a knowledge of good and evil adequate to form a basis of choice. According to the ancient but wonderfully meaningful story of the Fall, there was no sin in Eden until our first parents, discontented with their human lot and desiring to be "as God," ate from the tree of knowledge of good and evil. Such knowledge is at once our bond of kinship with divinity and our undoing. Not ignorance, but humble dedication of such knowledge as we have to God and action by it in accordance with his will, is the demand of our faith.

And in the fourth place, sin, according to the Christian frame of thought, involves at the same time relation to our neighbor and to God. As the Christian requirement of love links love of God and love of neighbor in a twofold great commandment from which neither element can be dropped, so sin against neighbor through lack of human love is a sin against God. The distinctive character of Jesus' ethics lies in the fact that for him religion and morals were all of one piece. To do the will of his Father and to serve those in need were for him not two requirements but one, a supremely costly but supremely joyous venture in self-giving love.

Put together these four requirements, and at least the outlines of the meaning of sin become clear. There is a sinful state of pride and rebellion against God from which not even the most saintly soul is wholly clear. There is culpable evil, such as anger, avarice, lust, killing, stealing, adultery, wherein one who is free to feel and to do otherwise chooses to obey evil impulses instead of good. There are sins of omission arising from moral dullness, flabbiness of will, and ignorance that is culpable because avoidable if we took pains to try to know. There are continuing large-scale sins against our neighbor, both the neighbor who is near and our fellow men around the world. These sins take many forms, but their basic roots are ethical insensitiveness and irresponsibility. These, in turn, center in self-love.

II

Throughout the history of Christian thought the idea of "original" sin has held a large place. Great sacramental systems have been created as channels of cleansing from it, and the fundamental difference between medieval and Reformation Christianity lay in differing convictions as to how God lifts its curse. Less prominent in theology, but always in the offing from the standpoint of personal living, has been the fear of committing the "unpardonable" sin.

For great numbers of contemporary Protestants, these are archaic and wholly meaningless concepts. I shall not attempt to defend all the meanings that have been put into these terms in the past. There is, however, a sense in which they refer to something permanent in human experience.

There is born in all of us, not original sin as a hereditary corruption passed on from Adam's guilt, but a biological tendency to self-centeredness. This egocentricity is as natural and unsinful in little children as is the organic impulse to eat or sleep or cry from discomfort. It is a useful endowment, not only for self-preservation, but for the growth of personality through the relating of all experience to the self. But such self-centeredness, though very necessary, is very dangerous, and in adult life it easily passes over into willful selfishness. If uncurbed, it becomes the self-love which is the root of all other sins and of most of our unhappiness.

So firmly do the tentacles of self-centeredness enmesh us that we cannot by will power break their hold. Whether selfishness takes the form of callous indifference or of positive self-seeking, being ashamed of it will not release us. Shame may be a step toward repentance, but it cannot of itself deliver us, and may serve only to enhance despair. God alone can free us. But can God? Only if we yield our wills to him and in repentance and faith lay hold upon his forgiveness. If we do not, our self-love is "unpardonable," not because God does not desire to pardon us, but because we do not make the commitment of faith which alone opens the way to his forgiving mercy. God cannot meet us if we block the path. The "sin of unbelief" is no theoretical rejection of God's existence; it is the deadlier atheism of preferring our way to his, of choosing to live by our own desires and standards to the rejection of his righteous will. If persisted in, it means the death of our higher life and of all that is potentially best within us.

The forms such self-love takes, in the ordinary events of living, are manifold. It shows itself in overweening desire to have our way regardless of the wishes or rights or needs of others; in the narrowing of interests to what immediately touches us; in thirst for personal recognition, compliments, and applause; in eagerness in conversation or action always to occupy the center of the stage; in jealousy of others who secure recognition or privileges or goods we want; in inordinate self-pity; in peevishness and petty complaint when things do not go as we would have them. These are, at best, unlovely traits when we see them in others. As indications that we love ourselves more than we love our neighbor or our Lord, they are evidences of sin so life-strangling that God alone can give release. They are the most potent and, indeed, the most common sources of the dark night of the soul.

When one goes to the Sermon on the Mount to see what Jesus considered important, one is struck with the difference between his standards and those which currently prevailed in his time, and still prevail in ours. It is not those who act according to the requirements of conventional respectability and avoid breaking the law who receive his approbation. The truly happy, the blessed ones, are those who in simplicity of spirit, in suffering, in humility, in aspiration for righteousness, in mercy, in purity, in peace, in steadfast devotion to high ends, seek after God and walk in his way. A legalistic ethic condemns such overt acts as murder, adultery, perjury, and aggression. Jesus put the emphasis in a different place. "Ye have heard that it was said to them of old time, . . . but I say unto you"—do not be angry, do not lust, do not be irreverent, do not retaliate, do not hate. In a word, do not let self-love master you.

We have said that the basic sins are ethical insensitiveness and irresponsibility and that these reduce to self-love. This is where the ethic of Jesus centers. "Ye therefore shall be perfect, as your heavenly Father is perfect" is not a text for an abstract and impossible perfectionism but a continuing challenge to try to see and act, within our limits, as a loving God sees and acts. To the degree that we fail to be as responsive as we can be to the call of God, we are guilty in his sight and condemn ourselves to a living death.

III

But what of the bearing of sin on the experience of the dark night?

There is one fact on which the psychiatrists and the theologians agree—namely, the devastating effects of a sense of guilt. Though opinions differ as to whether the way out is to try to deny the fact of sin or to accept one's sin and seek forgiveness, there is no question of the burden a sense of guilt imposes. There are those who think Paul was abnormal when he cried out, "Wretched man that I am! who shall deliver me out of the body of this death?" I do not know of anyone who denies that people do feel like that or that it is a terribly unhappy, soul-disturbing experience when it comes.

Guilt has various disrupting effects. For one thing, it begets fear. On the human level there is fear one may be found out, fear of social disapproval and perhaps of punishment, fear of loss of opportunity or security. However blithe one tries to be about it, there is a lurking fear of what the guilty act may bring to oneself. (This is why a lie detector works!) There is often also a gnawing fear of the consequences to others, as to one's family, for whom one feels concern. Since conscience is seldom wholly dead, there may be a paradoxical fear of evil consequences even to the person one has deliberately injured. All this is on the human, social plane; but if one is a religiously sensitive person who has not learned to take his sins to God and leave them with him, there is also a devastating fear of divine displeasure.

Fear is intimately linked with remorse. Remorse is a purgative emotion that leads on to repentance and thus to release. Fear is an inhibiting emotion; yet they are seldom clearly dissociated. They come so mixed that it is the rare individual who can drop his fear of consequences and maintain an attitude of true penitence. Short of trust whereby the guilty person, though acknowledging his guilt, surrenders his life to the keeping of another, it is impossible to banish fear. Without its elimination remorse is bound to be distorted—too little or too much, directed toward false ends, burdensome but uncorrective. This is why persons of sensitive conscience but without a deep-grounded religious trust often torture themselves with remorse far out of right proportions to the seriousness of their sins.

Guilt causes loss of energy and efficiency. It may have serious physiological effects through setting up emotional conflicts. Whether or not it causes bodily changes, it is bound to sap the nerve of effort through pre-empting attention and presenting a rival claimant for the effort that ought to go to one's job, or one's study, or to some other constructive end. (This is why in schools and colleges behavior difficulties and low scholarship so often go together.) Then, by a vicious circle, a sense of failure increases the sense of guilt and begets more failure. The belief that one has failed, whether in the framework of a human expectation unfulfilled or a duty to God disobeyed, begets an impotence that cuts the roots of motive power and leaves its victim inept, unhappy, and dismayed.

Guilt causes a sense of alienation and loneliness. This is true on both the social and the religious level. One who knows he has done something wrong begins to suspect that others know it too, and he becomes furtive and secretive. He thinks his friends no longer like or trust him. Rather than risk being charged with his offense, he curtails his social contacts and cuts himself off from help from friends just when he most needs it.

Though one seldom realizes just what is happening, a sense of guilt in a religious person dims the ardor of his approach to God, saps the roots of prayer, leaves him feeling alienated and alone. This is why the dark night is so often characterized by both a sense of spiritual bereftness and a real or imagined weight of guilt. Again a vicious circle intensifies the misery, for the guilty person feeling himself cut off from God by his unworthiness is the less able to find in God the grace that would loose his chains.

Put together these phenomena—corroding fear, a burdensome and often disproportionate remorse, the loss of positive incentive to constructive effort, and the loneliness of separation from human and divine companionship—and the only result is psychic disturbance of far-reaching proportions. A person in this state must have help or perish.

IV

We have been dealing above with guilt as a positive sense of wrongdoing. But, as we saw in the preceding section, sin can also take the form of a deadlier self-centeredness which breeds moral dullness, self-righteousness mixed with self-concern, complacency before evils that ought to be righted and work that ought to be done, jealousy and self-pity, overpowering desire for personal recognition, privilege, and preferment. What relation has sin of this sort to our problem?

The first thing to be said is that sin of this kind is not infrequently both the forerunner and the aftermath of the guilt ensuing from more overt sin. Lethargy, spiritual torpor, and "sins of omission" are not always linked with positive wrongdoing, but they often are. The problem is greatly complicated by the fact that the best people, as well as the worst, may have a sense of guilt that in its swingback breeds impotence and apathy.

Let us, however, assume that the reason for moral

dullness lies in a self-centered and unawakened will. One has never been stirred to think very far beyond himself and his own immediate circle of interests, and is callous to the needs and claims of others. For the greater part of humanity, what the *Theologia Germanica* graphically calls "the I, the me, the mine" is the main concern.

What happens in this all too prevalent situation is a dominant mood of self-seeking and a feverish quest for what one wants, alternating between dissatisfaction when one gets it and self-pity when one does not. It is such egocentricity which generates the chronic state of being "anxious for the morrow." Jesus said, "Be not anxious for your life, what ye shall eat, or what ye shall drink; nor yet for your body, what ye shall put on"; yet for hosts of persons this is the dominant concern that dwarfs all other considerations. For persons living close to the economic margin of existence such concern is unavoidable, and some thought for the morrow is obviously imperative for all. But the anxiety against which Jesus warned stands in direct relation to the self-seeking against which he counseled when he said: "Your heavenly Father knoweth that ye have need of all these things. But seek ye first his kingdom and his righteousness."

In the moral dullness which prompts self-seeking at the cost of complacency before the evils of the world, there is often no overt sense of guilt. But other intensely disturbing emotions ensue. Not only anxiety but envy, jealousy, anger, self-pity, and chronic discontent are the habitual accompaniments of self-centeredness. Stanley

Jones in his book *Is the Kingdom of God Realism?* presents many illustrations of the devastating physical as well as psychic effects of resentment, fear, self-centeredness, and guilt.[1] Selfishness may show itself in cold calculation or hot anger, in cynicism or flattery, in suavity or petty peevishness. But whatever form it takes to maneuver for its ends, to be a selfish person means, in the nature of things, to be a frustrated, unhappy person.

The Kingdom of God as set forth in the way of Jesus *is realism,* and there is a moral order in the universe, including our bodies, which does not let us flout it with impunity. St. Anselm was right when he wrote: "Should any man or bad angel be unwilling to submit to the divine will and rule, yet he cannot escape from it; for when he would escape from under the will that commands, he does but rush under the will that punishes."[2] This holds true whether with reference to the catastrophe of global war which engulfs a society mainly geared to personal and national self-interest, or to the individual who, seeking to exalt his own life and its private interests, loses life's richness in petty clamor and habitual complaint. The wages of sin is death, and we die—whether as a society or as single individuals—in those aspects of our being where the temptation to self-interest finds lodgment and diverts our living from God's way of service in love.

[1] See especially chapters v-viii.
[2] *Cur Deus homo,* Bk. I, chap. xv.

V

The bearing of the facts upon our problem is by now obvious. Among the many factors that may plunge one into the dark night, not the least is sin—not illness or maladjustment but culpable, unregenerate sin. This is found, whether in the form of overt guilt or selfish moral complacency, in all persons, including Christians. The only way its burden can be lifted is to face one's shortcomings, repent without despair, make such amends as are possible, and lay hold upon the eternal and encompassing mercies of God.

The way out is plain, but difficult. In fact, so strait is the gate and so narrow the way that, as we are told on highest authority, few there be that find it. Hence the morass of misery that engulfs our world. The only way to deliverance, for which there is no substitute, is unreserved surrender of the desires of the heart to God, and willingness *above all else* to be his servant. This does not mean for any human being sinlessness or unmarred happiness. It does mean victory over both sin and pain, and the power to live with courage, humility, and love.

Not sinlessness, but an ever-renewed victory over sin, is the central message of the Christian gospel. He who can say in an agony of despair, "Wretched man that I am! who shall deliver me?" can also say with an assurance born of triumph in Christ, "Nay, in all these things we are more than conquerors through him that loved us." To find such deliverance is perennially the most needful quest of the human spirit.

Chapter IX

The Practice of the Presence of God

WE SHALL NOW LOOK BRIEFLY AT CERTAIN OF THE classics of the devotional life to see how great souls of the past have been led through the dark night to the light of God's presence. If they found something authentic, we must try to find it. We shall glance at the work of four—not in every instance the greatest, but those whose message is most relevant to our problem.[1]

I

It is appropriate that we begin with St. John of the Cross. I do not propose to say as much about him as might be expected from having borrowed the title of his book.

St. John was the companion and younger contemporary of St. Teresa in the founding of the order of the Discalced (barefoot) Carmelite nuns and monks. This desire for reform in the direction of simpler and more austere living precipitated the wrath of the orthodox Carmelites upon them, and in 1577 St. John was

---

[1] *Augustine's Confessions* is the greatest spiritual autobiography since the New Testament. However, since his inner turmoil was ended by his conversion, we must pass him by.

148

imprisoned in the Calced Carmelite monastery at Toledo. Here, while living in a dark cell and subjected repeatedly to inhuman floggings, he composed a great poem, his *Spiritual Canticle*. Like the book of Canticles in the Bible, it reads on the surface more like erotic than religious literature. However, the Saint apparently meant by it to convey symbolically his conception of the approach of the Christian lover to God the Beloved.

Escaping from imprisonment, he wrote at intervals within the next ten years an extensive prose commentary on the poem. This work, the two parts of which are entitled *The Ascent of Mount Carmel* and *The Dark Night of the Soul*,[2] runs to 131 chapters and is full of penetrating observations on the pitfalls and glories of the religious life. It shows remarkable understanding of human nature as well as of mystical piety. Unfortunately, it stops short of telling what the modern reader is most anxious to know, which is how the soul actually becomes one with God.

We cannot do more than suggest the outlines of the Saint's approach. His main theme is the purgation of the soul to fit it for union with God. In *The Ascent of Mount Carmel* he presents the requirements of active purgation, that is, the cleansing from sin which man voluntarily undertakes through the help of God. The first stage is to pass through the dark night of sense, which is the mortification of earthly desire. But for

---

[2] *Spirit of Flame*, by E. Allison Peers, gives a readable popular introduction to St. John of the Cross, though the author says less of the dark night than one could wish. The best edition of St. John's complete works is edited by Peers and published by Burns Oates, London.

release from other baggage that would encumber it in the journey the detachment of the understanding is required, and the soul by faith enters the dark night of the spirit. The third stage, often called the dark night of the will, is a further renunciation of self through the purgation of memory and will. The night of sense is compared to the beginning of night, the point at which things begin to fade from sight; faith, to midnight, which is total darkness; and the third stage, to the dawn, which is near to the light of day and to God.[3]

So far the purgation, though costly, is by man's free consent. But in *The Dark Night of the Soul* the processes of passive purgation are traced. Here are found the misery and anguish, the doubt and despair of the Christian who, against his own understanding and will, is being purged by God and made ready for the transformation of perfection in love. So deep-seated, even in devout souls, are the sins of spiritual pride, avarice, luxury, wrath, gluttony, envy, and sloth, that God must take stern measures to eradicate them. No mere carnal sin, but the deadlier sins of complacency, self-righteousness, spiritual self-indulgence and display, "a sinful gluttony in spiritual things," are the most corrupting imperfections of the soul.[4] The Saint's contention is that the agony of the dark night is thus God's gift and a blessing in disguise. Throughout the rough journey the soul is being led through the dark by the loving hand of

[3] *The Ascent of Mount Carmel,* Bk. 1, chap. ii. The third stage is classed by St. John of the Cross as a continuation of the dark night of the spirit, though he is somewhat ambiguous at this point.

[4] Bk. I, chap. ix. In Bk. I, chaps. ii-vii, these sins are surveyed with great penetration.

God, though the traveler blinded and careworn is bereft of the sense of God's sustaining presence until the night is passed.

What shall we make of this? In the first place, one sees here a variation of the familiar mystical "ladder of perfection," with its three stages of purgation, illumination, and union. The mystic's initial requirement of moral cleansing is soundly based. It is written on high authority that the pure in heart shall see God, and, contrary to the common assumption, the great mystics have always had a profound moral concern. The second stage, which takes in St. John of the Cross the form of renunciation of the understanding for faith, is more debatable. Both understanding and faith we must have for true illumination, not a surrender of either. Too often the mystics conceived the life of the intellect as a barrier rather than aid to the devout life. The final stage of union, however arrived at, is baffling to most of us. As *communion* with God and the yielding of man's will to his, it is essential to the Christian life. As metaphysical *union* or even as perfection in the union of will, it is a difficult and somewhat dangerous concept. With due regard for the fact that the mystics have always considered the ecstasy of union so sublime an experience as to be ineffable, one cannot escape the suspicion that St. John of the Cross may have stopped short of describing it because he did not quite know what to say.

His interpretation of the passive purgation of the dark night presents deep insights and raises profound questions. No one has ever written with more discernment of the spiritual pitfalls that beset the path of devout and high-minded Christians. Their eradication, at whatever painful cost, is something for which gratefully to give thanks to God. Many have testified to this in retrospect. One may need to be blinded to discover the feebleness of one's faith, and there is a sense in which those are right who have seen in the dark night the working of God's holy purpose drawing them to himself. As in the other forms of pain—though this is the deepest and darkest of them all—pain is not its own last word. It may be God's word calling the soul toward light. It *is* God's word if the sufferer lets himself be drawn by it toward God's nearer presence and a purer devotion to his will.

This is not to say that the experience is to be prized for itself—much less be cultivated. As we can see in our time more clearly than did St. John of the Cross, it is sometimes the product not only of moral aberrations but of physical and psychic strains.[5] We must believe it to be God's will that these be avoided for oneself and prevented for others if this can be done without surrender of integrity. But when the dark night comes, we shall

[5] St. John of the Cross attempted to distinguish between the dark night as the act of God and the aridities which might proceed "from sins and imperfections, or from weakness and lukewarmness, or from some bad humor or indisposition of the body" (*The Dark Night of the Soul*, I, ix, 1). The marks of distinction he gives are that in the true dark night one finds no pleasure in anything created, is painfully conscious that one is backsliding, and has a constant rather than intermittent "embarrassment and dissatisfaction of the faculties." These seem to me inadequate criteria, presupposing greater differences in subjective manifestations than the facts warrant.

do well if, like the Saint, we can find in it by faith a path
that leads to the Mount of Vision.

II

We shall look for a moment at another, who had her
own troubles with the dark night, and who puts her
conclusions in somewhat simpler terms. I refer to Madame Guyon, friend of Fénelon, who a century later
than St. John of the Cross, practiced and wrote of the
devout life. Like him, she came into conflict with the
ruling powers for straying from the beaten ecclesiastical
path, and was for a time imprisoned. I shall cite only one
very suggestive passage in her *Spiritual Torrents*.

The different levels of religious experience are likened
to three rivers. There is the first class of souls

who, after their conversion, give themselves up to meditation,
or even to works of charity. . . . They do not cease to flow
from the source, but it is so feebly as to be barely perceptible.
. . . These rivers carry little or no merchandise, and, therefore,
for the public need, it must be taken to them. . . . The spiritual life of this class only thrives in proportion to their work.
If this work be removed, the progress of grace within them
is arrested: they resemble pumps, which only yield water
in proportion as they are agitated.[6]

Save for the reference to meditation, one recognizes
here the ordinary church member—and some preachers!
The second class

are like those large rivers which move with a slow and steady
course. . . . They are charged with merchandise. . . . Their

[6] *Spiritual Torrents*, chap. ii.

strength is very abundant; they are laden with gifts, and graces, and celestial favors; they are the admiration of their generation and numbers of saints who shine as stars in the Church have never passed this limit.

Why need they pass it? The answer is poignant:

And yet they are never really brought to a state of annihilation to self.[7]

The third class of souls are mountain torrents which, passing many precipices and abysses, move on to the sea to be lost in it.

And there, however poor, mean, useless, destitute of merchandise the poor torrent may have been, it is wonderfully enriched; for it is not rich with its own riches, like other rivers, which only bear a certain amount of merchandise or certain rarities, but it is rich with the riches of the sea itself. It bears on its bosom the largest vessels; it is the sea which bears them, and yet it is the river, because the river, being lost in the sea, has become one with it.[8]

Though the symbolism here is not that of the "dark night," the idea is the same. What the saints saw, after God had chastened them, was that they were now ready to carry great merchandise, not of their own gifts and graces or even of their own spiritual devotion, but on the boundless bosom of the Sea. This is an interpretation of spiritual union which has profound significance for the

[7] *Ibid.*, chap. iii.
[8] *Ibid.*, chap. iv.

Christian of every age. Only as we seek in humility to let God carry us can we carry our burden, whether of trouble or of rich merchandise for his service.

III

We turn now to the devotional classic which for the past five centuries has done more than any other book outside of the Bible to nourish the spiritual life of the Christian world. This is usually called Thomas à Kempis' *Imitation of Christ,* though it now seems probable that Thomas Haemmerlein of Kempen, near Cologne, was the copyist and not the author of the book. It is likely that it was written by Gerhard Groote, one of the company of Dutch mystics known as the Friends of God. But no one knows with certainty. Its authorship is shrouded in the anonymity appropriate to the humility that saturates the book and gives its piety a captivating, selfless charm.

Whoever wrote it, he had learned like Paul in the school of Christ how to be abased and how to abound. We shall pass over the many chapters that speak only of simple, unwavering trust and obedience to look at some that show remarkable insight into the painful depths of our problem.

The chapter headings themselves are suggestive. One finds, for instance, such titles as, "Of Lacking of All Manner of Solace," "Of Asking of God's Help and Trust in Recovering Grace," "That the Desolate Man Ought to Offer Himself into the Hands of God," "That Man Must Give Himself to Low Works When High Works Fail."

The best thing we can do is to cite a few excerpts.[9] To begin at the last title noted, we find this realistic but comforting word in which God speaks to the troubled soul:

As long as thou bearest a mortal body thou shalt find heaviness and grievance of heart. . . .
Then it is speedful to thee to draw thyself to meek and outward works and to take recreation in good active occupations, abiding my coming and the high visitation with a steadfast trust, and to suffer patiently thine exile and dryness of soul till thou be visited anew and delivered from all anxieties.[10]

Keep doing something worth while and wait patiently for God—no better occupational or spiritual therapy has yet been discovered!

The purgation of which St. John of the Cross makes so much is here also. In this passage the pronouns shift, and the author speaks to God about the desolate man:

But if thou withdraw thyself as thou art wont to do full oft, he may not run the way of thy commandments; but rather his knees are bound to knock his breast; for it is not with him as it was yesterday and the other day when thy lantern shined upon his head and he was defended under the shadow of thy wings from temptations falling upon him. . . .
For a little time let him be set little by, be meeked (humbled) and fail afore men, let him be broken with passions and langours, that he may rise again with thee in the morrow

---

[9] Quotations are from the "Everyman's Library" edition, which is based on the first English translation slightly modernized in spelling and syntax.
[10] Part III, chap. lvi.

tide of a new light and be made bright in heavenly things. . . .

Without thy counsel and thy prudence and without cause is nothing done on earth. Good is it for me, Lord, that thou hast meeked me, that I may learn thy laws and cast away elation of heart and presumption. It is profitable to me that shame and confusion have covered my face, that I may require thee to be my comfort rather than men.[11]

That God, not men, is not only the source of all true comfort but the measure of all our values is a dominant note of the book. But the long difference between God and man does not, as in some modern treatments, lead in the direction of despair. In a chapter with the very suggestive title "That a Man Must not be Thrown Down Too Much if He Fall in Any Faults" we read:

Why doth a little thing said or done against thee make thee sorry? It is no new thing; it is not the first, nor shall not be the last, if thou live long. . . . Thou canst counsel well and labour other men with wise words; but when a sudden tribulation cometh to thy gate, thou failest both in counsel and in strength.

Take heed to thy frailty. . . . At least suffer patiently if thou canst not suffer joyfully. . . . Restrain thyself and let nothing inordinate pass thy mouth that might be to the small and to the feeble an occasion of falling. . . . Grace returning again, the inward sorrow shall soon be made sweet.

Be mighty in soul and gird thee and make thee ready to more sufferance. It is not done idly if thou perceive thyself ofttimes troubled or grievously tempted. Thou art a man and not God, thou art flesh and no angel.[12]

[11] Part III, chap. lv.
[12] Part III, chap. lxii.

Even in quaint old English, so pertinent is this advice to our contemporary plight that one is tempted to keep on quoting. But citation from one more passage must suffice. The author apparently knew well himself what it meant to feel bereft of spiritual consolation, and was eager that none be cast down when this experience befell him. Thus he writes:

> This is no new or strange thing to them that are expert in the way of God: for ofttimes in great saints and holy prophets hath been this manner of alternation. . . .
> If it were done then with great saints, we, feeble and poor, ought not to despair, if some time we be in fervour and some time in coldness. . . .
> I have found no man so religious or devout that feeleth not some time withdrawing of grace or diminution of fervour.[13]

Stop here, and the words might inflate the ego by making the sufferer think he belongs with the saints and prophets! Or at best it would say to him, "Cheer up. Other good people have been as bad off!" But the author does not stop here. The chapter ends on a note which, like all the rest of the book, links comfort with challenge and challenge with warning:

> "He that overcometh," saith our Lord, "I shall give him to eat of the tree of life." Heavenly comfort is given that a man should be stronger to sustain adversities; temptation also followeth lest man be proud of the gift; the devil sleepeth never and the flesh is not dead.
> Wherefore, cease not to array thee to battle: for both on the right hand and on the left are enemies that never cease.

[13] Part II, chap. ix.

IV

Of all the humble, devout souls who have left their record there is none who speaks to us more aptly than Brother Lawrence. We shall, therefore, attempt at somewhat greater length to interpret his message.

Three centuries ago there was a cook in a French monastery by the name of Nicholas Herman. He did nothing more spectacular than to live a simple, radiant life of fellowship with God. He did not even write a book. He wrote some letters, and sixteen of these, with four accounts of conversations with him and some maxims, have come down to us to make an immortal classic on *The Practice of the Presence of God*.[14]

The problems which beset the inner life of the religious person are nearly constant from age to age. One must come to terms with oneself, in particular with temptations to pride and subtle forms of selfishness, to complacency, anxiety, irritation, and discouragement. One must adjust the spirit to the body and its claims. One must meet the strains put upon us by other people, both those who annoy us and those whose need demands our help. One must adjust the life of work to the life of prayer. All of these adjustments, and not the last only, require the constant reorientation of life toward God.

In these vital areas of the relations of the soul to its own evil impulses, to its body, to the social situation, and to the demands of a vocation, Brother Lawrence has much to teach us. His record does not cover the

[14] This is available in an inexpensive edition (8 cents each, 5 cents a copy for five or more) from the Forward Movement, 412 Sycamore Street, Cincinnati, Ohio.

whole gamut of life's demands; for he knew nothing of domestic conflict, his intellectual interests were soon satisfied, and his life within four monastery walls was far removed from the anguish and clamor of global war. It would be easy to say that in a situation so simple he could do what we cannot. Yet I, for one, cannot read him without feeling that here is something so authentic that he "speaks to my condition."

The starting point of Brother Lawrence's spiritual victory is often overlooked. Externally the details of his life are meager. He tells us "that he had been footman to M. Fieubert, the treasurer, and that he was a great awkward fellow who broke everything," but that desiring to be made to smart for his awkwardness he had entered the monastery, only to find nothing but satisfaction in that state.

Regarding his spiritual odyssey he is far more explicit. During the first ten years of his attempt to practice the presence of God he seems to have suffered from spiritual dryness or the dark night of the soul. In what he says of these ten troubled years, it is easy enough to read between the lines a sense of spiritual defeat, inability to find power in God or a warm awareness of his presence, abnormal self-condemnation and self-distrust, doubt as to whether salvation was for him. But he hung on, even when it seemed that "all creation, reason, and God himself" were against him. The joyous outcome he states with touching simplicity:

When I thought of nothing but to end my days in these times of trouble and disquiet (which did not at all diminish the trust I had in God, and which served only to increase my faith), I found myself changed all at once; and my soul, which till that time was in trouble, felt a profound inward peace, as if it had found its center and place of rest.

It is this "profound inward peace" that makes the dominant motif without which we should never have heard of him. A sentence epitomizes his life: "When the appointed times of prayer were past, he found no difference, because he still continued with God, praising and blessing him with all his might, so that he passed his life in continual joy."

This repose of soul affected his vocation. His kitchen work, to which he had naturally a great aversion, became easy, and he was able to find dignity and greatness in the most trivial act. Among the best-known passages are those in which he speaks of turning the cake that is frying in the pan or picking up a straw from the ground for the love of God. He had abundantly a sense of calling in his work, the loss of which is one of the most serious aspects of our present economic life.

His religion had its effect upon the body. Not only was serenity written in his face as a witness to his faith, but it gave him a transcendence over bodily ills such as our feverish age might well covet. He says "that he expected, after the pleasant days God had given him, that he should have his turn of pain and suffering; but that he was not uneasy about it." Apparently such days came. In his old age he writes, "I have been often near expiring. . . . I did not pray for any relief, but I prayed for strength to suffer with courage, humility, and love." He goes to the root of a most important matter when he says, "If we were well accustomed to the exercise of the presence of God, all bodily diseases would be much alleviated thereby."

His total adjustment to life was the product of his practice of the Presence. Though he lived in a simple environment, he knew what it was to have conflicting demands impinging on him from several directions at once. Apparently he was able to take it without the nervous tension that is the curse of our time, even among Christians. At the end of the Fourth Conversation appears a vivid snapshot of his personality:

He was never hasty nor loitering, but did each thing in its season, with an even, uninterrupted composure and tranquillity of spirit. "The time of business," said he, "does not with me differ from the time of prayer, and in the noise and clatter of my kitchen, while several persons are at the same time calling for different things, I possess God in as great tranquillity as if I were upon my knees at the Blessed Sacrament."

Who is there who would not like to have such "an even, uninterrupted composure and tranquillity of spirit"? Is it possible to have it, pressed upon as we are by many matters? That we have known some Christians who maintain it even under the most staggering burdens demonstrates the possibility. Let us see how Brother Lawrence found it.

1. He let his ends determine his procedures. The end of all his actions, he tells us repeatedly, was to do everything for the love of God, "seeking him only, and nothing else, not even his gifts." Such singleness of purpose is

the clue to the fact that he could continue to trust God even during the first ten troubled years. Faith can survive much distress and difficulty, and even the dulling of the sense of God's presence, if the soul is oriented not toward its own states but toward God. It is when the Christian loves the gifts of God, including the spiritual gifts, more than he loves God that darkness engulfs the soul.

There is a distinction here that we in our time need to make. We pray legitimately for certain needed material gifts, such as daily bread and physical health. We pray for events earnestly desired, such as world peace and the safe return of loved ones from battle. We pray for courage and strength to accept if necessary the denial of these petitions. Here most of us stop, assuming that spiritual blessings are the supreme object of prayer. What Brother Lawrence saw was that the chief end of man is not to enjoy God or even his richest gifts, but to glorify him. It is when God and his Kingdom are sought first that "all these things" are added.

2. He made his set times of prayer continuous with the life of devotion. Though the heart of his religion was praise and submission to God in the midst of his labors, he did not give up his regular periods of prayer. Both have their place, in our lives as in his. Without the discipline of regularity, our praying becomes so free that before long we are free from prayer. Without a sense of the presence of God in the activities of the common life, prayer tends to become an emotional luxury, a thing apart from the world of commonplace duties and demands in which most of our hours are spent.

The ordinary Christian today is barren enough in his prayer life of both types. Those who have a regular time of daily prayer are probably in the minority in our churches. The scantiness of our praying is the chief reason for the fact that there is often so little difference between those who call themselves Christians and those who do not. But if regular times of prayer are the exception rather than the rule among Christians, the life of continuous devotion in the midst of other activities is so rare as to raise the question whether it is possible.

Is it possible? What does Paul mean when he enjoins us to "pray without ceasing"? Is the experience of Brother Lawrence, or of Frank Laubach as recorded in *Letters of a Modern Mystic,* so abnormal that we can only admire without emulating it? And if we could do it, would it not mean a division of attention curtailing our effectiveness in practical matters?

The answers become clearer when we observe how Brother Lawrence did it. He was not in conscious prayer all the time. But he tried always to be responsive to God's "inward drawings." To increase this receptivity he uttered short prayers in the midst of his business "by such words as love forms upon these occasions, as for instance, 'My God, behold me, wholly Thine: Lord, make me according to Thy heart.'" When an occasion arose that required the practice of some virtue he addressed God saying, "Lord, I cannot do this unless Thou enablest me," and received strength more than sufficient. When his mind wandered he refused to be disquieted, but drew it back and again fixed his thought upon God.

With prayer as the dominant mood or attitude of one's

life, the practice of the Presence becomes habitual. This, I take it, is what happened to Brother Lawrence. Not the continuous utterance of vocal petition, which obviously would be impossible if one were doing anything else, but the surge of the soul Godward, is the heart of the experience. How frequently one can give conscious attention to God differs with individuals. All of us can go further in this direction than we have.

3. Brother Lawrence understood the limitations of human nature, including his own. One must think of God "the most he can." One must "accustom himself, by degrees, to this small but holy exercise." Speaking of an overardent sister (of whom there are plenty of modern counterparts), he writes, "She seems to me full of good will, but she wants to go faster than grace. One does not become holy all at once." He apparently expected and had dry times, for he speaks of the need of fidelity "in those times of dryness, or insensibility and irksomeness in prayer, by which God tries our love to him."

There is nothing which reveals the basic sanity of his religious experience more than his attitude toward his own failures. There is a tendency among religiously sensitive persons to condemn themselves to the point of discouragement, if not despair, at their shortcomings. Repentance, which is essential to any true religion, can easily pass over into a kind of remorse which is a devastating form of self-centeredness. Not so with Brother Lawrence. "When he had failed in his duty, he simply confessed his fault, saying to God, 'I shall never do otherwise if Thou leavest me to myself; it is Thou who must hinder my falling, and mend what is amiss.' After that he gave himself no further uneasiness about it."

4. He found enough to do for others to keep him from self-concern. We are told little about his dealings with the rest of the monastery family. In one of the Conversations is a note to the effect that, finding so much comfort and blessing in the practice of the presence of God, he desired to recommend it to others, and that they were more influenced by his example and the "sweet and calm devotion" of his appearance than by his arguments. A great person does not talk much about his services to others, and is silent about the souls he has won.

However, the letters show beyond question that Brother Lawrence was an intercessor and a master of the art of counseling. All but one of the sixteen end with the assurance of his prayers, and all are full of understanding and comfort. There is in them no condemnation, but much of humble witness, encouragement, sympathy, direction as to how to pray and what to pray for. One cannot read them without knowing that Brother Lawrence had the channels of his life turned outward, and that, being fed from God, they could not help watering the dry places in the souls of others. With all his praying, he was unmistakably an extrovert.

What shall we make of him—this humble, happy figure of three centuries ago? Could he have foreseen that he would become an immortal, it would have seemed so incredible to him that one wonders whether his tranquillity could have stood the strain! Yet he did nothing except what any of us can do. He was not a fanatic or a saint, but a simple Christian who talked with God and let God carry his troubles for him. There is good psychology and sound sense as well as good religion in his words, "Everyone is capable of such familiar conversation with God, some more, some less. He knows what we can do. Let us begin, then."

Chapter X

Joy for Mourning

IN THE SIXTY-FIRST CHAPTER OF ISAIAH APPEAR SOME great words. The Spirit of the Lord God is upon him, says the prophet,

> To comfort all that mourn
> . . . .
> To give unto them beauty for ashes,
> The oil of joy for mourning,
> The garment of praise for the spirit of heaviness;
> That they might be called trees of righteousness,
> The planting of the Lord, that he might be glorified.[1]

The "spirit of heaviness" is, I take it, the prophet's name for the phenomenon of the dark night. Apparently he believed that it was a distortion of the soul, to be remedied only by a recovery of the "garment of praise" which the soul attuned to God finds native to it. Any modern idea of such heaviness as being due to physiological or environmental factors, and thus to be taken care of by change of circumstances, would have been foreign to Isaiah's thinking.

What we have said throughout is that the garment

[1] Isa. 61:2-3 (A.V.).

168

of praise must replace the spirit of heaviness, joy supplant mourning, through the power of God. But in the process some near-at-hand and this-worldly matters must be set right by God's help. What we are dealing with is essentially a religious problem requiring a religious solution; it is also a problem of adjustment requiring treatment through action based on a God-given insight and moral imperative. Let us see, then, how these factors come together.

If a person in a state of nervous depression wants to escape from the tension that is tearing his life asunder, certain requirements must be met. Among these are (1) willingness to be helped, (2) the correction of any physical causes or environmental factors that can be ascertained and changed, (3) the acceptance as inevitable of those factors that cannot be changed, (4) an object of devotion and interest outside oneself, (5) the gaining of perspective, and (6) confidence that life has meaning.

How are these requirements related to what the Christian gospel demands and offers? This must be our final inquiry.

I

The first requirement for emergence from depression is the willingness to emerge. In one sense, this is easily met, for it is a state of acute unhappiness in which nobody likes to remain. In another sense, it is the hardest of all requirements to meet, for paralysis of will is the crux of the issue. In a comparable problem, that of alcoholism, it is significant that the group of cured victims who call themselves Alcoholics Anonymous make their first requirement for helping anyone that the person be willing to be helped.

It is at this point that the Christian doctrine of divine grace, when rightly understood and interpreted, has great relevance. The Christian gospel is not that we save ourselves by finding God. It is that God finds and saves us when we let him. The God who is ever waiting to impart himself and his infinite resources has made us not mechanical puppets but co-operating persons who must say yes at the "threshold of consent." Barriers not of our making may block our wills at many points and cut us off from a sense of God's presence. Yet nothing but our own indifference can cut us off from the *desire* to find him! As we seek him, he finds us.

It is the Christian's rightful faith that, however dark the night, God's love surrounds us. Whether we find him near or far, or cry out in anguish but hear no answering word, we still can know that God has not forsaken us. When we are assured that God ceases not to love us, we can watch in patience through the night and wait for the dawn. Then as God finds us and speaks to our waiting spirits, peace and power flow into our lives.

The release from heaviness may come all at once, as one makes the surrender of faith and feels a great burden lifted from his soul. Dr. E. Stanley Jones records such an experience in his *The Christ of the Indian Road* when after months of nervous depression he found physical health and spiritual power through committing himself completely and finally to God's keeping. So it has happened with many others. Doubtless something like that happened at Pentecost to the first Christians, when an influx of power through the Holy Spirit transformed their lives. But we ought not to be troubled if it does not happen in just that way to us. To use William James's phrase, there are many "varieties of religious experience"; God does not run us all into one mold. With some, the release is less sudden and the search for God must be many times repeated. Yet, if with all our hearts we truly seek him, we can know that *God finds us* and gives rest to our souls.

Prayer, then, though it seem unanswered, is not futile. It is the channel by which God can release the tensions which hide him from our sight. But only if we pray in patience and are willing to wait for his appearing. He who would cast off heaviness through faith must be willing to say, "I will arise and go to my Father." And he must be willing to say it, not once, but many times.

II

To overcome depression, one must do what can be done to locate and correct its causes. It is good Christian doctrine that prayer requires works for its completion. Many physical and social causes of the spirit of heaviness could be removed by intelligent effort, and it is blasphemy to expect God to work a miracle in our behalf if we continue in ways of living that head straight toward nervous exhaustion.

To canvass these in some detail was our main purpose in chapters six and seven. However, it may not be out of place to review them here.

Most of us know how to live better than we do live. Too much work or too little play, lack of sleep or fresh air or exercise, eating too much or too little food or the wrong kind, too many stimulants or sedatives, the loneliness that comes from too meager social contacts or too much jostling in the crowd, organic or functional illness, particularly glandular disturbances and persistent infections, pressures and strains from displaced organs in the body—these and many other abnormalities upset one's mental outlook and make all of life seem dark. Most of these are fairly simple and this-worldly matters. Yet they have profound spiritual consequences.

Other more complex problems, such as family tangles or economic insecurity or distasteful drudgery or racial tensions or, with the coming of the war, the engulfing of all humanity in new and chaotic conditions, have less chance of being readily adjusted. But in almost every instance *something* can be done. It is inherent in the Christian gospel that in these matters something *must* be done—if not for ourselves, then certainly for others. The grace of God comes to us, and through us to other men, as we make channels for it by the breaking down of physical and social barriers to the abundant life.

III

A third requirement is to accept without inner rebellion that in the situation which cannot be altered. Our Christian faith requires that we do what we may and endure what we must.

There are conditions so unalterable that neither prayer nor human effort will avail to change them. Death comes

172

to all. Its coming can be retarded but not forever, and the disease that is its precursor may have to be accepted as incurable. The limb cut off or the eye plucked out will not grow again. Our lost youth will not return. The economic resources once so readily available may be gone —gone not to be recovered in our lifetime. When the shadows thicken and our loved ones die, they will not come back in the loved familiar form. When the night of war comes upon the world, separations, sufferings, and the surrender of much that is precious in the old familiar ways must be accepted as inevitable.

To accept such factors as inevitable is not easy. When one brings himself, with God's help, to the point where he can accept them, he has gone a long way toward mastery. But still more difficult and more important is the need to *accept oneself.*

No one knows how many millions of people have become derelict personalities, unhappy and permanently frustrated, because they were unwilling or unable to accept their limitations. Our limitations ought not to be prematurely accepted, for many of them can be overcome. Their conquest makes heroism and high adventure. But some must be accepted, not supinely but humbly. To know that one has, not superior, but mediocre talent; to know that education and experience have fixed limits to what one can do and that one cannot by wishing reverse the past; to know that a vocational choice, however short of the ideal best, is fixed; to know that in all probability one will never achieve distinction in a coveted field; to know that, however much one expends himself, he has neither strength nor wisdom to do all the good that needs to be done—in short, to lay one's limitations as well as one's gifts before God and let him transform inferiority into humility, this is the way to valiant, effective service. To work well in restricted circumstances is to achieve far greater success than to thresh the air in wider spheres.

It is not only in major matters but in small that one must learn to accept himself and his situation. It is in the triumphant acceptance of life's inevitables that our Christian faith has its most visible testing. But it is not an unusual happening for one to meet triumphantly great times of testing and yet "go to pieces" in both nerves and Christian fortitude under the daily strain of a nagging member of the household, or of a nagging pain that will never be fatal to life but is constantly a barrier to life's enjoyment. One often feels ashamed that, having endured great crises, he seems unable now to endure a continuing succession of minor irritations. Whether we ought to feel shame depends on many things. If self-pity obsesses us, as it is altogether too prone to do, the sooner it is banished the better for all concerned. Yet for balanced judgment one needs to remember that long-continued minor irritations become major matters. If they cannot be eliminated they, too, must be accepted with as much good grace (which means God's grace) as can be brought to bear upon them.

IV

The sufferer, to secure release, must look beyond himself. Our Christian faith provides an object of devotion and loyalty which, in Professor Whitehead's trenchant words, "stands beyond, behind and within the passing flux of immediate things." This is why Christian faith and action are the supreme corrective to nervous fretting and depression. For depression is primarily a form of introversion—of turning one's gaze inward in abnormal self-concern. Its forms are manifold—fear, worry, loneliness, suspicion, jealousy, resentment, inferiority, confusion of soul. Yet all stem from too much absorption in self, and this is at least partially the case when the object of worry is not oneself but a beloved person belonging to oneself. Whether the spirit of heaviness takes the form of anxiety, self-pity, or self-condemnation, or, as frequently happens, of all of these at once, the most disrupting mental activity one can engage in is too much introspection.

To the degree that one is captured by a loyalty and devotion that lifts one's soul up to God and out to his fellow men in service, his reward is great. To "look up, and laugh, and love, and lift" is a simple but potent injunction that may be more effective than many dollars' worth of psychiatry! Or, to be more explicit, this advice which the wise psychiatrist will probably give anyway may be had for nothing by taking it from the insights of the Christian gospel.

But not for nothing, for one must take it to have it. It is often the most difficult task of a counselor to lead the sufferer to the point where he can be captured by a great and commanding devotion. It cannot be commanded from without or added on as an accretion to life: it must command the whole person by capturing him from within. Herein lies the paradoxical freedom of losing life to find it, the liberty that comes through surrender to the God "in whose service is perfect freedom."

Here again, in small matters as in great, the principle of fulfillment through self-giving holds. If one will glance back at the case histories recorded in an earlier chapter, one will note in how many instances help came from the assumption of useful work—the amount limited, perhaps, but the responsibilities real. There are some cases of nervous exhaustion which demand complete rest; there are more in which idleness means introversion, and opportunity for the mischief which Satan proverbially puts in idle hands.

There is "a freedom that makes us mad." [2] If one has a family or friends to love and work to do, however irksome the details involved, let him rejoice that God has given him such saving responsibilities. If he has not, *let him find somebody at once*—today, within this hour—for whom he can do some useful service.

V

To get rid of depression one must get perspective—a sense of what is important and what is unimportant. It is, of course, one of the most characteristic symptoms of depression that the sufferer loses his normal perspective. This is why his moods and actions are so hard for his family and friends to understand, and why he

[2] See the very suggestive chapter entitled "Too Much Freedom Makes Us Mad" in Rollo May's *The Springs of Creative Living*.

is so often berated for making mountains out of mole-hills.

There is no simple rule to follow by which to enable oneself or another to see life in its true proportions. Sometimes such clarification comes best in direct counseling, if censure which induces anger and shame and thus raises still more dust can be eliminated. Sometimes it comes best through a more objective approach, such as a sermon or a book or an article loaned to be read. The value of personal counseling lies both in the illumination of issues and in the contagious spiritual health of the counselor. The value of the more objective method is that the sufferer is free to take for himself what he needs instead of being prompted to reject what some-one else thinks he needs.

A word may be in order here for the person who must counsel the person in depression. There are few things we do more poorly—not so much because of culpable insensitiveness as from a baffled sense of helplessness. Yet there are few things more necessary. Everybody needs someone—whether professional counselor, member of the family, pastor, or friend—on whom to cast part of his burden if he is to cast it fully upon God. It may be possible to have a victorious sense of God's sustaining presence apart from this human medium, but not many do. Even Jesus, to gird himself for Gethsemane and Cal-vary, needed the quiet intimacy of the home at Bethany.

Naturally, the counselor does not wish to say the wrong thing and do more harm than good. There is no single *right* thing to be said in every circumstance, but some cautions may be interposed. One ought neither to

177

coddle nor to condemn the sufferer, for he needs to rid himself of both self-pity and self-condemnation. Though some appeals to the will can and must be made, a normal exercise of will power ought not to be demanded. ("It is precisely what one tries hard with that is sick.") Don't worry! Buck up! Snap out of it! Act like a Christian!—it is doubtful whether these easily spoken bits of advice ever yielded a one per cent return. (Ask yourself whether *you* ever stopped worrying because of being told to!) Any oft-repeated formula, unless voluntarily accepted by the sufferer as a slogan, gets mechanical and tends to become an anathema. There is cold comfort in being told that there is really not much the matter, for many people are worse off. If, then, the comforter proceeds to tell with what fortitude he has borne similar distress, the sufferer has perforce to grit his teeth and pray for grace!

There is a place for humble witness to the power of good. There is a large need for clarification of causes, effects, and all the circumstances bearing on the situation. One needs to be a patient listener, with the discernment to know when the sufferer is being helped by unburdening his spirit and when the repetition of the tale of trouble is only intensifying self-pity. Often the best thing a wise counselor can do is by sympathetic understanding to show in himself something of the love of a God who always understands—who knows our frame and remembers that we are dust.

VI

The victim of depression must find meaning in life.

Without such meaning, his personality has no organizing center, no worthy object of devotion, no light for seeing beyond the immediate issues of the moment, no power for spiritual victory. It is the undercutting of a sense of life's meaning that is responsible for most of the neuroses of our time.

The Christian faith imparts meaning to life. A living faith that is centered in the God revealed in Christ takes our chaotic, disorganized selves, with their crude jumble of pleasures and pains, and knits them together into a steadiness and joy that can endure anything with God. The meaning of the cross is that sin can be forgiven, pain overcome, by the victory of God—a victory that is both within and beyond this earthly scene. The lives of countless Christians in this and every age bear witness to power through faith that in Christ we see what life is for.

That this victory of faith repeatedly occurs is not man's achievement only. Supremely, it is God's gift. Yet it is man's task to lay hold upon God's gift—in faith, with hope, by love. However dark the night that surrounds or dwells in us, no man need be without hope. And as Paul once put it, though the whole creation groan and travail in pain together until now, we are saved by hope.

This calls for far more serious attention to the inner life of devotion than in our hurried lives we commonly give. Many Christians, even Christian leaders, have yet to learn to pray in any but surface fashion. It takes discipline to maintain a regular time and place for prayer; it takes dedicated willingness to be able, like Brother

Lawrence, to respond at all times and places to God's "inward drawings."

As to the form of prayer, much latitude is possible. Effective praying requires both alertness and quiet receptivity. Fortunately, God requires of us no one posture or form of diction; however halting the words, if we speak in faith and listen in patience, his Spirit will respond. Yet God merits that we approach him with "comely praise." One may well use some of the great old prayers of the Church, beautiful in their simplicity and mellowed with centuries of expression of human need. One must learn to formulate for himself, and perhaps for others, both the timeless divine assurances and the contemporary needs that confront us. Some pray best with a devotional manual, others are impeded by it. "Try it and see" is an excellent principle. What everyone needs to do is to find for himself the most effective manner of praying, and practice it. The ultimate test of right praying is not its verbal form but the willingness to ask everything "in Christ's name"—in the spirit and manner of Christ.

As we must learn to pray in order to discover life's fullest meaning, so we must learn to read the Bible. It is one of the tragedies of our time that the Bible is a closed book to so many who might otherwise find from it life-renewing power.

To read the Bible fruitfully, we must let it speak to us. "It is not a riddle for you to solve, nor a magic charm for you to use, but a message for you to hear." [3] This

[3] From a pamphlet entitled *A Preface to the New Testament* by Paul S. Minear. This is so valuable a compilation of suggestions as to how to read the Bible that an excerpt is reprinted by the author's permission in the Appendix.

means learning all one can about the historical setting of the various books and the manifold circumstances which, through more than a thousand years, were bringing it into being. But it means also letting God speak through it as if he were speaking directly to you. One should not be troubled at failing to understand some passage; others will leap out from the page as if meant precisely for you. Sometimes one will want to read an entire book at a sitting and feel its sweep. Again, and usually for devotional purposes, it is better to read only a few verses at a time and let one's mind dwell unhurriedly on their meaning.

Not only in church but in the family or with a congenial group it is a fine experience to read the Bible aloud together and listen to its beauty. (It ought to be read *well* if this is done!) Use the King James Version for its majestic cadences, the American Standard Version for clarity, the Moffatt or some other modern translation for freshness and pungency. It is a great pity that there is not as much memorizing as formerly of the deathless passages in the Bible. There is no better antidote for insomnia or nervous fretting than to repeat to oneself certain of the psalms or other great biblical assurances.

Prayer and the reading of the Bible are, of course, not the only channels for the discovery of life's meaning through Christian faith. The Church, as the carrier of the gospel, exists for this purpose. As the ongoing fellowship of those bound together by a common loyalty to Christ, its very existence points to the power of the Christian message to transcend the centuries and speak vitally to every age. Not all words spoken in church are vital; but even in the most barren of services there is something to be found in the hymns, the prayers, the scripture, the spoken message, the act of corporate worship, which can quicken the heart and bring light to the soul.

It is a high art to conduct public worship with dignity and power; it is a different but equally important art to participate in it worshipfully. One must overcome the temptation to be a passive or critical spectator and make himself a part of the worshiping group. One must learn to screen out what, if anything, is irritating in the human aspects of the service and center attention on God and his truth. One must let oneself be lifted into God's presence; one must inwardly be still enough to hear God speak. Such discipline is not easy, but it is of great reward.

The finding of joy for mourning—or, in the terminology of this study, the conquest of the dark night of the soul—is basically a matter of laying hold upon the means of grace. Traditionally, the "means of grace" have been the sacraments of the Church. It is unfortunate, but true, that to great numbers of Protestants these sacraments now have little meaning and convey little power. This fact calls both for more meaningful interpretation of the sacraments and for the use of other channels as effective means of grace.

Of these there are many. One may find God and his light through the beauty and order and quiet peace of nature, though it is to be doubted whether one ever finds God through nature who has not first found him through more personal channels. One may find him through art and music; through great literature, particularly biography; through the funded wisdom of the ages. One may find him through human fellowship and through the daily duties of one's vocation. Of the last two we have spoken at length; of the others much might be said.

There is one means of grace that never fails. This is incarnation in life of that which God imparts to men through Christ. If one can do nothing else to help a troubled soul, one can treat him with understanding, sympathy, and Christian love. Then religious health, fed by its sources in Christ, becomes contagious. Though the sufferer may not be able to describe what has happened, life looks less dark and its burdens less crushing. The full victory does not usually come all at once. But one goes forward, growing in power to endure and to say with Paul, "We are pressed on every side, yet not straitened; perplexed, yet not unto despair."

Such deliverance is the ever-repeated triumph by which God saves men and lifts them to strength. There are not many things today that the world needs more!

To help suffering, struggling souls find the way to God is a work to be done, not by ministers only, but by all Christians. It is a work to be done, not by guess and not by a blueprint, but by an insight into the nature of God and of the persons he has made in such baffling but majestic intricacy of soul.

Helping people to find joy for mourning means an ongoing witness to the gospel in life as in word, without self-righteousness or self-praise or cant. It calls for earnest prayer, and for the giving of instruction in how to pray and what to pray for. It calls for guidance of the troubled soul into rewarding work, whether in his vocation or the church or the community. It requires in the counselor the sympathy that rarely censures and never berates the fainthearted for his lack of faith, the sinner for his sin. It requires the depth of understanding that will avoid the dispensing of superficial advice or the peddling of conventional panaceas couched in pious phrases. It requires the courageous and clear-visioned intention to seek first the Kingdom of God and his righteousness, however counter to it the currents of the day may run.

This is no easy undertaking! No one can do it perfectly. At best, we shall judge ourselves to be unprofitable servants. But we shall judge the service to which God calls us to be of supreme importance, and we shall keep on trying.

In these days of despair, the most important thing that anyone can do is to refuse to be desperate and to help others to find power in God, who is our refuge and our strength. To comfort those that mourn, to give to them beauty for ashes, the oil of joy for mourning, the garment of praise for the spirit of heaviness—who has a greater task? Let no Christian think lightly of his calling.

Appendix

A. Selected Bibliography

I

ON RELIGION AND HEALTH

Allport, Gordon W. *The Individual and His Religion: A Psychological Interpretation.* New York: The Macmillan Co., 1957.

Boisen, Anton T. *Out of the Depths: An Autobiographical Study of Mental Disorder and Religious Experience.* New York: Harper & Bros., 1960.

Clinebell, Howard J. *Mental Health Through Christian Community.* Nashville: Abingdon Press, 1965.

Doniger, Simon (ed.) *Healing: Human and Divine.* New York: Association Press, 1957.

Fosdick, Harry Emerson. *On Being a Real Person.* New York: Harper & Row, 1943.

Hiltner, Seward. *Religion and Health.* New York: The Macmillan Co. 1943.

Hofmann, Hans. *Religion and Mental Health.* New York: Harper & Bros., 1961.

Oates, Wayne E. *Religious Factors in Mental Illness.* New York: Association Press, 1955.

Stein, Edward V. *The Stranger Inside You.* Philadelphia: Westminster Press, 1965.

Weatherhead, Leslie D. *Psychology, Religion and Healing.* Nashville: Abingdon Press, 1951.

Wise, Carroll A. *Religion in Illness and Health.* New York: Harper & Bros., 1942.

II

ON PSYCHOTHERAPY

Frank, Jerome D. *Persuasion and Healing: A Comparative Study of Psychotherapy.* Baltimore: Johns Hopkins Press, 1961.

Frankl, Viktor. *Man's Search for Meaning: An Introduction to Logotherapy.* Boston: Beacon Press, 1962.
———. *The Doctor and the Soul.* New York: Alfred A. Knopf, 1965.
Fromm, Erich. *The Art of Loving.* New York: Harper & Row, 1956.
———. *Psychoanalysis and Religion.* New Haven: Yale University Press, 1959.
Guntrip, Henry. *Psychotherapy and Religion.* New York: Harper & Bros., 1957.
Horney, Karen. *Our Inner Conflicts.* New York: W. W. Norton Co., 1945.
Oates Wayne E. *The Religious Dimensions of Personality.* New York: Association Press 1957.
Outler Albert C. *Psychotherapy and the Christian Message.* Harper & Row, 1954.
Roberts, David E. *Psychotherapy and a Christian View of Man.* New York: Charles Scribner's Sons, 1950.
Rogers, Carl R. *On Becoming a Person: A Therapist's View of Psychotherapy.* Boston: Houghton Mifflin Co., 1961.
Stern, Edith M. *Mental Illness: A Guide for the Family* (revised edition). New York: Harper & Bros., 1957.

III

ON PASTORAL COUNSELING

Bruder, Ernest E. *Ministering to Deeply Troubled People.* Englewood Cliffs, N. J.: Prentice-Hall, 1963.
Clinebell, Howard J. *Basic Types of Pastoral Counseling.* Nashville: Abingdon Press, 1966.
Hiltner, Seward, and Colston, L. G. *The Context of Pastoral Counseling.* Nashville: Abingdon Press, 1961.
Jackson, Edgar N. *Understanding Grief.* Nashville: Abingdon Press, 1957.
Johnson, Paul E. *Person and Counselor.* Nashville: Abingdon Press, 1967.
Leslie, Robert C. *Jesus and Logotherapy.* Nashville: Abingdon Press, 1965.

Appendix

Oates, Wayne E. *The Revelation of God in Human Suffering*. Philadelphia: The Westminster Press, 1959.

Wise, Carroll A. *The Meaning of Pastoral Care*. New York: Harper & Row, 1966.

B. How to Read the Bible[1]

The New Testament is addressed to you. It is not the special possession of priests and scholars, monks and missionaries. It was written by the people and for the people; and not for all people in general, but for individual men and women like yourself. It is not a riddle for you to solve nor a magic charm for you to use, but a message for you to hear.

The New Testament is a library. Its shelves are lined with the earliest writings of men called Christian, writings which reflect every aspect of their dramatic existence. These writings tell the strange story of God acting in the life of a man called Jesus. The story centers in the awful death of this man on a cross; it tells of God's choice of that crucified man to reveal his purpose and his power; it points to the revolution which that cross produced in human hearts and in human history; it arrests the reader with a tribute to the freedom and faith, the courage and hope which that cross released. Christians preserve these books because, once knowing them, they cannot forget them. Once confronted by the strange man on the cross, they cannot escape him.

Yet the store-house of New Testament treasures does not open with just any key. Many readers find baffling puzzles, an uncharted jungle of strange ideas and attitudes. They do not know where to start, how to find what they need, what to listen for, how to translate ancient stories into modern meanings. If you belong to this group of readers, the following suggestions may serve to direct you in your use of this library.

SOME SIGN-POSTS

1. Read when you are alone, when you have time to think seriously about yourself, when you want to understand your own

[1] From *A Preface to the New Testament* by Paul S. Minear. Reprinted by permission of the author.

life and death, when you reflect about the source and goal of that inner center which you call yourself.

2. Read quietly and slowly, not as you race through the daily newspaper. Don't always read at the same pace; get in step with the material you are reading. At times each verse will require pondering; at times a paragraph or chapter is the natural unit of thought. "Not snap-shots but time-exposures" should be the rule.

3. Read with *all* your senses alert and active. Don't be content with seeing the words; speak them aloud so that you can *hear* them. Taste them for saltiness of wit or irony. Picture the setting for each separate scene. Get the feel of the atmosphere. Ask constantly the question: "*Why* was this written, how did early Christians use it, what did it mean to them?"

4. Reading is a two-way conversation in which you participate. Visualize yourself as a character in the stories. Talk back, raise questions, disagree. These writings, when they are understood, always cause conflict.

5. Express your reactions by underlining, notes in the margin, question marks, exclamation points. Cut out pages for your diary if you wish; few books are more easily replaced and none more important to have where and when you want it.

6. When you find a statement that strikes fire, copy it and repeat it aloud several times. Jot down the chain of thought it starts. Let it lie near the surface of your mind for a whole day as a magnet to your thoughts.

7. The only reason for conversation is to discover a word *not your own,* to hear *another* voice. Forcing your prejudices upon another's lips kills the friendship. If you do what many people do—tell the New Testament what it must say—you lose a friend.

8. What should you do when you strike a snag? Don't be surprised. Every library has such riddles. Move on to a section more clear and interesting. Remember that you are not studying a text-book but reading personal letters from Christian friends of other lands and generations.

9. First and last, the New Testament halts you with this claim: "God has here a word for you." You will not hear it if you read only for information or enjoyment as, for example, when you scan the Reader's Digest. But if you see yourself as the object of God's action, then you will hear him speaking. Upon his will you are dependent. He has a purpose for you; read to grasp that purpose.

10. When He speaks, your immediate inner response is all-important. When he condemns, bow in penitence. When he offers help, rivet your hope on that assurance. When he commands, obey. Tomorrow's promise is reached by the path of today's faithfulness. Reading the New Testament is an invitation to participate in God's activity in history. The epic told in these pages is an unfinished story which your life helps to complete.

C. How to Pray[1]

All sincere Christians at times feel like saying as the disciples did to Jesus, "Lord, teach us to pray." [2] It is so difficult, yet so vital, an art that one feels baffled before it.

Like any other art, it is impossible to reduce it to rules. To do so would make it a technique and not an art. But there are certain principles to observe.

First, *prayer must be centered upon God*. The Lord's prayer begins with an act of adoration. The psalmist wrote, "I have set the Lord always before me." [3] Anyone who does not do this is not praying —he is simply rearranging his own thoughts. But it is not enough to begin with some formula of adoration or thanksgiving. You must feel your own littleness before God's greatness: you must genuinely feel grateful and receptive. To induce this mood, it is helpful to think over your blessings and your own shortcomings. Then self-searching and petition fall into their rightful places, and you can

---

[1] Reprinted from the author's *Religious Living* (New York: Association Press, 1937). Used by permission of the publishers.

[2] Luke 11:1.

[3] Ps. 16:8.

ask God to help you in anything of importance to you. It does not matter greatly about the sequence or form in which the words shape themselves. The less you think about that, the better. But it matters much that God be put foremost in your attitudes.

Second, *prayer must be natural.* This means that some people pray best in forms familiar through long experience and others through petitions framed anew on each occasion. You have to discover in which way you can do it most readily. Variation is helpful —pray sometimes by using memorized prayers, sometimes thoughtfully read a prayer from some good collection, sometimes shape your own. No prayer made up by another will touch your life in everything, for no one else has exactly your experience and your needs. Yet the experience of others—particularly in the great prayers used by the Church for centuries—will help you as your own grows. You need especially to be on guard lest prayer become merely a mechanical repetition of words. The moment you find this happening, change to some other form.

Third, *prayer must be unhurried.* This does not mean that it must be long drawn out. Most of the great Christians I know are very busy people. There is danger of being so busy even about good works that God gets pushed out. To keep God at the center of one's life requires frequent renewal of power through prayer. But such renewal is not measured by the amount of time it takes, rather by the degree to which one is able even for a short time to have relaxed and unhurried communion with God. One can pray inwardly at any time and anywhere—in a subway or on an athletic field. But one prays best either alone or with understanding friends. To avoid neglecting to pray, it is best to have a time-habit and a place-habit. This is so important that it is worth great effort, in spite of the hurry of life and our lack of privacy.

Fourth, *prayer must be intellectually sincere.* It is a mistake to try to pray to a God you think does not exist, or to pray for something you think cannot possibly happen. This does not mean you should stop praying if you have some doubts. Often, to pray is the best way to get the personal depth of religious insight before which your doubts will flee away. But if prayer seems a "hollow mockery," do not go on letting it mock you. Get a book and read what some philosopher of religion whom you trust says about it. Decide whether you agree with him. Then pray according to whatever framework of belief seems to you intellectually satisfying. Do *not* try to philosophize while you are praying, for you cannot have a spiritually receptive and an intellectually analytical attitude at the same time. There is need for analysis before and after, but to try to analyze while you are praying is ruinous. Stop praying infantile prayers addressed to an elderly gentleman in the sky if you have been doing so, and pray with emotional and intellectual maturity.

Fifth, *prayer must combine alertness with passivity*. While you are praying, you ought not to work too hard at it. To do so is to screw yourself into a tension which prevents being receptive—and receptivity is of the essence of prayer. But neither ought you to relax so much that you fall asleep, or into a day-dream. Praying is not *strenuous,* but it is *serious* business.

Sixth, *prayer must be accompanied by active effort*. It is a very irreligious attitude to pray and expect God to do all the work. There may be situations, as in serious illness, when there is nothing more you can do. At such times, to pray and then in calmness to leave the outcome to God is the best procedure. But almost always you can do something. In illness, to pray and not to give adequate medical care would be unwise and unethical. The same holds everywhere else. You need to pray for wisdom and strength for your own remaking, and then set yourself to it. You need to pray for others and set yourself to helping them. Some people do not believe in praying for other people, but I think it is required of us both for what it may lead to in itself and as a stimulus to our service.

Finally, *prayer must be based on intelligent trust*. This means that you ought not to pray for things which God cannot give you without upsetting his laws or doing contradictory things. This does not forbid you to pray for essential material things, for "daily bread" is an important part of life. But it will not come to you miraculously, and you should not expect it to. It is far more important to pray for strength and courage to accept deprivation with spirit undaunted than to pray for the specific things you want.

The greatest prayer ever uttered was one spoken in a garden, "Nevertheless not my will, but thine, be done." [4] Every petition should be made in this spirit. What matters supremely in prayer is that God be exalted and that you be brought to a life-transforming willingness to follow his way.

[4] Matt. 26:39; Mark 14:36; Luke 22:42.